Hurt

Nicholas T. Spatafora

R & Q
Press Inc.
📖

Published by Reed & Quill Press, Inc.
New York, NY

ISBN: 9780981756400

Printed in the United States of America

FOREWORD

There are a growing number of people seeking to bridge the gap between psychology and religion; thus, many are turning to psychotherapists who have a theological background and incorporate the spiritual into their practice.

A recent conference of the APA was held, addressing the long-held premise that psychology and theology conflict with each other. Psychology and religion are not mutually exclusive, however. They are not as vastly opposed to each other as the theoretical society once believed. Psychoanalysis, for example, has its origins in Eastern religion, which attempts to understand one's Self through investigation and inquiry, tracing his thoughts, feelings, attitudes and behaviors to their source. Likewise, dream analysis, which is generally attributed to Freud, was actually employed in biblical times when dream interpreters were chosen to analyze the King's dream in *The Book of Daniel* some 2500 years ago. Although an atheist himself, Freud encouraged forgiveness, as did Christ, lecturing about the physical and psychological dangers of harboring anger and resentment. Similarly, optimistic thinking is not only modeled by the therapist in psychotherapy but is also an essential component of most religions that view conflict and struggle as an opportunity for spiritual enhancement. I myself incorporate spiritual principles into my practice, especially in recent years, to meet the growing number of clients who seek a psychoanalytical and spiritual balance. To say that one is independent of the other negates the validity of both.

Hurt is unique in its theoretical and theological approach to recovery, personal awareness and spiritual growth. I think you will appreciate the book's splendid blend of psychology and spirituality, as well as its versatile writing style, which furnishes concrete information and rhetoric, illustrating arguments and concepts with quotations, examples and open-ended questions, along with the writer's personal touch of wit and humor.

Sincerely,

John V. Staton, CSW, NCPsyA

John V. Staton, CSW, NC Psy A.

To my family, friends and colleagues who supported and
encouraged me during a difficult time.
To John Staton, who was always there for me.

To my wonderful and loving wife Judy,
who never left my side.

Contents

PREFACE

It happened on Labor Day morning 2001 only months away from a wedding that I would never see. It was supposed to be another of our cherished road trips for two, viewing the autumn leaves and scenic mountains of New England's countryside. Instead, Maine was to set the stage for the most devastating experience of my life, one that would change its course drastically. In fact, it nearly cost me my life.

It was on April 13, 1998, that we met for the first time. I remember it well. I was on sabbatical from school, finishing up my graduate work at Hunter College in New York City, when I answered a New York Magazine personal ad—"Single White Female, 42, seeks SWM." We met on the corner of McDougal and Bleeker Street in New York City's Greenwich Village. It felt as if I had known her all of my life, and before long, I knew that I was experiencing love for the first time.

The next three years were like a fast, ephemeral, wonderful dream. We went everywhere and did everything together. I was so happy; I thought that she was, too. I had done more for her than I had for any other woman. A man who had once denounced his friends for putting their women before their family and friends was now doing the same thing to his. What was worse; I was putting her before myself.

She began hinting at marriage. I knew that it would just be a matter of time before I proposed, and I was a confirmed bachelor, who prior to meeting her, would not even entertain the possibility.

On the eve of Memorial Day 2001, under a crystal clear midnight sky overlooking the glistening Baltimore Harbor, I presented her with the ring. It was picture perfect. But I was scared. I never thought that I would muster up the courage to ask anyone to marry me, and neither did my family and friends who said, "You'll never go through with it." But I did go through with it to her shock and disbelief. She accepted.

I look back at the next three months that followed. It is all a mysterious blur to me now. Everything happened so quickly. She started to become very critical of me, picking arguments and finding petty reasons to reject every wedding hall and every house that I liked. Was she stalling for time? Was this her way of railroading me out of her life? In the end it was, for when I gave her carte blanche on the wedding hall and house in August, she ended the engagement and finally the relationship itself. The nightmare was about to begin.

Having previously given up my apartment in Queens, she invited me to move into her apartment with her until I had found a place of my own. Perhaps there was still a chance, I thought, and despite the advice of family and friends, I moved in on October 1. Within hours, she began to place inordinate and excessive demands on me, complaining about everything that I did, finding fault and criticizing me relentlessly. At this point, it finally became clear to me that she really did not want me in her life anymore and that it might have actually been a long time coming. Love is blind; though, and still I could not accept losing her.

November 2001—Reality struck me like a freight train. I was quickly slipping into depression. I lost all shreds of dignity, spending my last days pleading with her to give the relationship another chance. I was desperate, completely devastated and shivering, like a lost and frightened child. She did not waive, shed not a tear or displayed any signs of compassion or concern. Instead, she suggested that I leave right away. This was my "fiancée," a woman with whom I had shared three years of my life, made love and with whom I was planning a wedding and future. Now she no longer wanted to have anything to do with me. I do not claim to be the innocent babe of the woods; I have my faults like everybody else. But I was good to her and never assaulted her with so much as an unkind word.

It was a cold November morning when she finally said goodbye. I was disposed of like trash in a receptacle. I was trembling and weeping profusely. She tried to cushion the blow by insisting that it was better off for the both of us. Still grasping onto a glimmer of hope, I refrained from doing anything regrettable. Any hopes of winning her back quickly perished. The months that followed were unendurable, and I would spend the next three years of my life suffering from a depression that words cannot even begin to describe. My family, friends and colleagues were deeply concerned, and I truly believed that my days were numbered. The pain was just too unbearable. Yet something deep inside refused to succumb to an overpowering compulsion to take the easy way out of the indescribable misery from which I was suffering.

Then Providence and an angel in my corner brought John Staton into my life. John was a Godsend, for without this man, I would never have been able to survive the emotional pain and anguish with which I was confronted. John was available twenty-four hours a day, seven days a week. He returned my calls without delay, whether they were in the mid hours of the night or regardless of where he was. Not once did John tell me that he had no time for me, and even when my health provider neglected to provide for him, never did he fail to provide for me.

Inspired by John, I began writing *Hurt* on January 1, 2003, still in the depths of a serious depression. What started out as a diary and a few personal pages of comforting words of wisdom and advice would eventually evolve into an organized, researched compilation that would not only benefit me but also be of help to others. John was truly instrumental, supporting my ambition and efforts to see this book to its completion, and it was his inspirational guidance that prompted me to embark on a life-altering writing endeavor that was waiting to happen.

Time finally lifted the cloud that had engulfed me for what seemed an eternity, and severe arthritis sadly forced John into an early retirement. I would make intermittent telephone calls to John for occasional advice, a chat and to keep him abreast of the book's status.

My final call to John was a disheartening one, for it was during this brief telephone conversation that he broke the news to me that he was very sick. For the first time since I had known him, he would no longer wish to receive any correspondences. The months progressed quickly, and the final completion of *Hurt* would soon become a reality.

It was a cold, bitter encounter with reality, walking through the door of my Flushing apartment early Friday evening after work, tearing at the returned USPS parcel indifferently stamped "DECEASED." It had been addressed to: John V. Staton, CSW, Psy A, the first published copy of *Hurt*, with a personal inscription written on the inside cover by its author, thanking him for all that he had done and for being an angel on his shoulder. I wanted so much for this exceptionally special man to witness the final completion of this painstaking five-year-long undertaking, an achievement in which he himself was instrumental. His name sharing the book's cover with mine was to be my thank you and tribute, one that I know would have made him proud.

John, you shall forever remain in my heart, and to you I shall always be indebted.

Forever grateful,
Nick

First I was afraid
I was petrified.
Kept thinking I could never live
without you by my side.
But I spent so many nights
thinking how you did me wrong.
I grew strong.

It took all the strength I had
not to fall apart.
Kept trying hard to mend
the pieces of my broken heart.
And I spent oh so many nights
just feeling sorry for myself.
I used to cry.

I'm not that chained up little person
still in love with you.

I Will Survive
(Made Popular by Gloria Gaynor)
Dino Fekaris & Freddie Perren

INTRODUCTION
From Despair...

INTRODUCTION: From Despair...

AFTER CROSSES AND LOSSES, MEN GROW HUMBLER AND WISER. BENJAMIN FRANKLIN

Y ou have been disposed of, dismissed, abandoned, betrayed. It feels as if you were kicked in the teeth. *She* is the one who should be feeling guilty and sorry for *you*, yet *you* are the one carrying the burden. Mom's told you for years to find someone nice such as yourself. Your parents never approved of your choices before, and they had a bad feeling about this one too, even though she was mom's twin and dad's duplicate. Friends noticed peculiarities. They too had bad vibes, said you could do better. You had your doubts also, but wanting to believe that you had found your soul mate, you went against your better judgment and remained in an abusive "relationship" on *his* terms, predetermined to end *by him* after you had served your purpose. You worshiped the ground that he walked on–and he knew it, exploited it. He made promises that you would keep. She cleverly had you believing that you were the King, the Queen, when you were nothing more than a court jester. When your time was up, she gave you the gate, suddenly, unexpectedly and ruthlessly. You felt orphaned, homeless and desperate. To mask her deceit and absolve herself of her guilt, she made you the scapegoat, choosing a firearm from an arsenal of lame loopholes that she'd had stored from the beginning, ready to railroad you out when the time was right. Being conscientious and gullible, you bought his lies and took on *his* sins in addition to "yours." You cried out in vain for compassion, mercy, forgiveness and a second chance–to get kicked– again. On the surface, she feigned love and concern while secretly eating it up inside. Adding insult to injury, you have been prohibited from making further contact with the illusion whom you have been duped into loving because your unjust feelings are intangible. Paradoxically, she looks like the victim, and you look like the villain.

Further contact is illegal, euthanasia is illegal, crimes of passion are illegal, and she and the law label you as "pathological" when your only crime is being sensitive, loving and justifiably devastated. You have no other choice but to swallow it, let time heal, grow, learn many invaluable lessons from the experience, discover that you were mislead, realize that she outranked you only by your love for her and thank your lucky stars that you are unmarried–to him.

The Things which hurt, instruct.
Benjamin Franklin

FOR MY DAYS PASS AWAY LIKE SMOKE,
AND MY BONES BURN LIKE A FURNACE.
MY HEART IS IN ANGUISH WITHIN ME,
THE TERRORS OF DEATH HAVE FALLEN UPON
Me.
FEAR AND TREMBLING COME UPON ME,
AND HORROR OVERWHELMS ME.
MY HEART IS SMITTEN LIKE GRASS, AND
WITHERED;
I FORGET TO EAT MY BREAD.
BECAUSE OF MY LOUD GROANING
MY BONES CLEAVE TO MY FLESH.
I AM LIKE A LONELY BIRD ON THE HOUSE
TOP.
I EAT ASHES LIKE BREAD,
AND MINGLE TEARS WITH MY DRINK.
MY SOUL REFUSES TO BE COMFORTED.
I AM SO TROUBLED THAT I CANNOT SPEAK.
THOU HAST CAUSED LOVER AND FRIEND TO
SHUN ME;
THOU HAST MADE ME A THING OF HORROR
TO THEM.

PSALMS

From one thing, another is born. Laura Resnick

Abandonment by a significant other can be a devastating and crushing blow to one's integrity and security, unleashing a Pandora's box of very intense and painful emotions. Depression, sorrow, rage, resentment, guilt, shame and fear can rear their ugly heads in the wake of a separation, and since no two personalities or circumstances are alike, the duration of the healing process following an abandonment trauma is dependent upon the individual. A sudden surprise abandonment by someone with whom you had prepared to invest your heart and future, never to be seen or heard from again, is far more traumatic, for instance, than a gradually deteriorating relationship mutual for both parties and may require a longer healing duration. If you have had a history of broken relationships, for example, losing someone a second or more times around can be even worse than the first. *Because of our cellular memories which have been left within us by our heart*, says Dr. Paul Pearsall, *every time we physically or mentally end a relationship, we are recycling through the ending of every relationship we have ever experienced* (180). We are also *re-experiencing grief from infancy when love loss was totally unbearable,* asserted E. Michael Holden, M.D. (Primal Page). Thus, one cannot compare himself to others, take heed of those who offer conventional time parameters for expected recovery, criticize or judge himself for exceeding some convenient six-month-to-one-year rule of thumb. For some it takes months, for others years. Do not despair, however, for as Benjamin Franklin once said, *calamity is the criterion of integrity*, and the intensity of your pain may be indicative of some much needed introspection and change, which only now have been prompted. Emotional distress indicates problems that need to be recognized and addressed sooner rather than later.

The objective of *Hurt* is to mitigate your pain and expedite your recovery. It is holistic, drawing from the scientific theories of psychology, the healing power of therapy, the inspirational wisdom of *The Holy Scriptures* and the experiences of over two hundred individuals with whom I have either researched or corresponded personally. One need not ascribe to a particular religious sect to appreciate or benefit from the scriptural texts herein or challenge these references from a purely scientific stance, as the information contained within this manuscript is universal, whether one is a devout Christian or a pragmatic Freudian.

You have been traumatized. Tears of sadness endlessly flow day and night. It is unrealistic to expect the anguish of such shattering an experience to vanish within one to three months or from exposure to one book, inspirational speaker, analytical session or clergyperson; however, through extensive biblical and psychological research, interviews and correspondence, therapy and a devastating three-year bout of my own, I have blended seven of life's most fundamental precepts that will reduce the pain of abandonment considerably and achieve the ultimate goal of recovery in as quick and reasonable a fashion as possible. The chapter synopses that follow will provide you with a brief summarization of the scope and content addressed within the text. It is my sincere belief that the pages contained herein shall minimize your pain and expedite your recovery so that you can begin to live life fully once again.

1. Take Responsibility
2. Understand It
3. Do Not Personalize
4. Be Thankful
5. Reach Out–You Are Not Alone
6. Forgive and Forget
7. Let Time Heal

CHAPTER I: Take Responsibility

"I should have known better!" Play with matches and you are going to get burned. Webster's defines responsibility as *a state of accountability for a personal decision* (Merriam-Webster 1062), in this case, the liability or risk that one assumes when developing or prolonging a relationship with a partner who from the onset exhibits undoubtedly even subtle indications that this partnership would not be to the other's interests or would it sustain. Responsibility in no way implies blame on the part of the abandoned for having contributed to the termination of the relationship, yet one cannot blame his assailant solely for confiscating his wallet after knowingly walking a dangerous street after dark.

Ray's former fiancée not only duped him into believing that a wedding was only months away, but she also mislead her colleagues, allowing them to throw a dinner celebration for the two of them within three weeks of canceling the engagement. We allow ourselves to be deceived. We meet people who lie compulsively, individuals whose intentions are nothing more than to stay with us for an indefinite period of time before they decide to move on to somebody new. *We read the world wrong and say that it deceives us,* according to philosopher Rabindranath Tagore, and it is in fact *not her love but the lover herself who is deceived* in this illusive mind game, adds George Santayana (Lewis).

This chapter examines five types of risky and terminal relationships and relationship choices with unhealthy and incompatible people whom you may be encountering, holding you accountable for developing and/or extending potentially destructive relationships, and applies Freudian psychology to explore and understand conscious and subconscious motives behind your choices.

1. Personal Diversity
2. The Unorthodox
3. Abusive People
4. Users/User Relationships
5. Affairs and Other Safe Arrangements

MY COMPANION VIOLATED HIS COVENANT.
HIS SPEECH WAS SMOOTHER THAN BUTTER,
HIS WORDS WERE SOFTER THAN OIL,
YET THEY WERE DRAWN SWORDS.

PSALM 55:20-21

> Jen leaves Rick for another man after dating him for four months. Rick is hurt and hopes that she will change her mind. Jen is rejected by her new fancy and returns to Rick one month later. He is overjoyed. He and Jen continue the relationship from where they had left off. She leaves Rick a second time for someone else, only this time a year later, blaming him with a petty excuse to justify her decision. Rick is now devastated. He feels victimized and guilty.

Rick could mitigate his victim mentality considerably–which attributes power to Jen–by taking responsibility for allowing her back into his life and prolonging a precarious situation with an untrustworthy person. In other words, he should have seen it coming. If we were to examine the relationship in retrospect, then we would recognize clues indicating that it was just a matter of time before Jen would abandon Rick a second time. Perhaps Rick initiated most of the telephone calls, conversations and affection. Jen might have phoned or dated Rick infrequently, affording her the time and opportunity to pursue other people. She might have had an apathetic demeanor, not having had a stake in the relationship to begin with or concerned with Rick's whereabouts in her absence. Love is giving, and if Rick did most of the giving, getting little in return, then this too should have been a sign to him all along. These indications start early on and may be subtle. If one were to make a written or mental list of them, however, then her involvement with a detached, self-centered or even abusive partner would become apparent.

Love does not end, and lovers do not separate. Love is unconditional, and except for self-preservation from acts of domestic violence and mistreatment, men and women are bound to each other in a marriage. Love is not abusive, and each partner is responsible for treating the other with dignity, care and respect. Love does not manipulate, threaten or intimidate (Montana). A lack of respect signifies a lack of love, and emotional or physical abuse has no place in a relationship. There is never any basis for a power struggle, and in genuine love, conflicts of individual interests should never come at the expense of the relationship. Love is not arrogant or rude, irritable or resentful. It is not jealous or boastful. It does not rejoice in the wrong but rejoices in the right. Love is patient and kind. It is long suffering. It bears all, believes all and endures all. Love does not behave indecently, look out for its own interests, become provoked, or does it keep account of injury. Love never fails; it does not end. It is not the money that you fail to make, the job that you do not hold, the car that you cannot afford to drive or the mansion which you never owned that destroys relationships but a reflection of one's own fickle, selfish and ephemeral nature. *A true companion is loving all the time* (Pr.17:17).

You were vulnerable to getting involved with someone who could hurt you. If you were to fold a piece of note paper into five columns, listing the undesirable characteristics of five close persons in your life, for example, friends, former mates and family, then you would likely discover three to five common traits from among these individuals.

> It is not an enemy who taunts me—
> then I could bear it;
>   But it is you.
> We used to hold sweet converse
>   together.
>   Psalms 55:12-14

Each of us perpetuates relationship patterns, whether they are choices in mates, friends or confidants, and it usually takes a traumatic event such as this, as well as the help of an analyst, for these patterns to be exposed. You might have been consciously or subconsciously seeking a casual or temporary involvement with an abusive or disinterested person. If you are always rejecting that sweet, shy and unattractive librarian who goes to all lengths to help you in favor of the knockout, narcissistic and arrogant cashier, then you shall continue to fall victim to selfish, abusive and manipulative individuals who will continue to use and abandon you. Make an honest assessment. If your recent man or woman seemed to be more interested in "making love" rather than love itself, then others from your past were probably similar and more than likely prone to affairs and multiple partnerships. In all likelihood, you have probably attracted and have been attracted to others similar who came previously; thus, you are answerable not so much to divorce, separation or the breakup itself but to subjecting yourself to a sort who would disappoint you ultimately. Taking responsibility for getting involved and allowing one's self to be placed in a no-win, vulnerable position reduces the likelihood of getting involved with someone such as this again and prevents future heartbreaks. You must recognize and put an end to this destructive cycle, and then a healthy and permanent relationship with a man or woman who truly has your best interests at heart will be more likely to ensue. By acknowledging the truth and taking responsibility, you will also reduce a considerable amount of the anger and resentment that you may be harboring toward your former partner by acknowledging your role in developing and perpetuating an ephemeral situation with a person who leaves much to question.

He behaves much as your father. She is the spitting image of your mother. *Understand it.* Explore and understand the subconscious motives behind your choices in people. According to Sigmund Freud, *it is the lifelong compulsion of the mind to relive early emotional traumas from even pre-infancy and seek out those with whom we can play out these circumstances in a never ending vain attempt to find closure for unresolved issues* (Felluga). A woman who witnessed her mother being abused by her father or experienced abuse as a

Know thyself.
Socrates

child herself, for example, may seek out a man with whom she can reenact the experience and avenge herself or her mother. Such a woman is likely to lead another person on, setting him up for a letdown ultimately. In the scenario described earlier, Jen might have had the conscious or subconscious ulterior motive of hurting Rick for a misdeed left unpunished from childhood; thus, she might have sought and capitalized on one of his flaws to justify hurting him in her own passive-aggressive behavior pattern. Rick, being unaware of this, is likely to self-recriminate to Jen's satisfaction. She will then play out this pattern with others until they too are left hurt and befuddled. Familiarity is also addressed, our being blinded to undesirable characteristics of people who exhibit many of the traits of our parents and authority figures. Rick might have been oblivious to certain abusive and manipulative tactics employed by Jen, perhaps because these might have been characteristics exemplified by many others in his life.

The Stockholm syndrome provides a concrete explanation as to why people often remain in abusive and unhealthy relationships (The Peace Encyclopedia). Akin to the hostages in Stockholm, Sweden in August of 1973 whose lives were spared by their captives, an abused woman, for the sake of argument, may choose to remain with her battering spouse because he has demonstrated intermittent gestures of love and kindness, all a manipulation, along with his verbal and physical outbursts or because time has blinded her to inappropriate actions and behaviors that are far more obvious to others (World Book, Inc.).

We begin to understand the motives behind the patterns that we perpetuate with the people to whom we have availed ourselves over the years and their similarities to our adult figures from childhood. Given his need to please even a woman who could not be pleased, perhaps like his mother or older siblings, it is very likely that many other significant people in Rick's life were also the unappreciative, manipulative, hurtful and hard-to-get types, and unless he begins to acknowledge this harmful pattern for himself, then he will be more than likely to continue to draw other people into his life who will take advantage of and hurt him eventually. Because of his familiarity with abusive figures and his own lack of self-worth, he is also likely to spurn people who are good-natured and genuinely interested. In this chapter, several cases involving individuals and their unhealthy relationship patterns are discussed.

CHAPTER II: Do Not Personalize

"I don't know what *I* did but whatever it was *I'm* sorry!" Rick feels compelled to buy into Jen's unfair and unfounded accusations. Our critical familial and societal upbringing and its incessant demand for perfection often leave us prone to guilt and self-deprecation and usually at the expense of our self-recognition and self-respect. This commonly shared problem, which is also largely a by-product of an abusive kinship, is amplified following a rejection by a significant other. It is a natural component of an abandonment trauma to make personal the other's disapproval of us, and the greater we esteemed them, the greater we personalize. This pattern is unavoidable regardless of your degree of self-confidence, self-esteem or personal integrity (Messina). We internalize the rejection, incorporating within complete guilt and blame for what has happened. We compulsively berate ourselves for all of our shortcomings, which we assume alienated our partner, instead of choosing to acknowledge our many attributes and the numerous gestures of love and devotion that we offered. Instead of recognizing Jen's shortcomings and her role in the demise of the relationship, Rick will readily scan his mind for every fault and every example of misconceived inappropriate behavior that he exhibited while with Jen and his own imperfections at the expense of acknowledging his qualities and perhaps recognizing his sense of conviction and his loyalty to her. Rick is human; he is going to make mistakes.

Self-deprecation and guilt feelings of culpability for imagined offenses or from a sense of inadequacy, however, can be reduced in intensity and duration if one has a stronger, more secure sense of self and self-worth; thus, Rick can liberate himself from or at least minimize these harmful tendencies by removing the stigma of self-reproach and considering the source of his accuser. A tree is known by its fruit, and it should be evident that Jen's actions suggest a woman who is fickle, probably having played out this pattern with other people prior to him, and who will undoubtedly continue to do so with others. It also implies like habits with the world at large. Most of us have given condolences to the needy, newly separated who suddenly take a renewed interest in our company only to vanish from our lives once again after they have found another relationship.

As if being unjustly criticized and blamed for their failure and inability to commit to a relationship is not insulting enough, do not punish yourself relentlessly by faulting and doubting yourself, too. Apologizing for the actions and behaviors of others is something that you may have always found yourself doing. Unless you were habitually unfaithful, repeatedly malevolent, insensitive or disrespectful toward her family and friends without legitimate cause, then you might in fact be vastly blowing things out of proportion, making a mountain out of a molehill, and envenoming your soul undeservingly. Regret may indeed be a rational emotion here, but guilt clearly is not.

Perfection is freedom from fault or defect (Merriam Webster 1062). Nobody is exonerated from either, and expecting one's self to be the exception to the rule merely perpetuates the need for it. All too often we blame ourselves for what our "partners" did as if their actions were somehow appropriate and justified, despite the profound legacy of pain and misery that we alone are left to deal with. We bear the weight of the world upon our shoulders, taking upon ourselves the burden of regret for not having done a better job, pleasing them and for falling short of that impossible goal called "perfection," while removing this burden from theirs. You may not yet be cognizant to the bizarre and mysterious buttons that might have been pushed. If you want to reprove yourself for something, then do so for getting involved with this person in the first place or for not getting out of it sooner (Messina).

Rejection is not personal. People do not reject you; they only reject their image of you, an image that only they have created in their own personal schemas and imaginations. Your former partner's behavior makes more of a statement about them than it does about you. Their behavior about your behavior also speaks about them and not about you. You are aware that after all of these years and all of those first date rejections that just because you could not appeal to one person did not mean that you would not capture the fondness of others inevitably. Being turned down did not make you repugnant or loathsome, and it did not define you as a person. The refusal certainly was not your first, or would it be your last (FitzMaurice).

Abandonment by a former lover can wreak havoc on our self-confidence and emotional security, especially if either was poor or lacking prior to the separation, and the intense and sudden shock of a rejection can bring to their knees even the most secure and self-confident among us (Messina). Rick has probably lost sight of his capacity for love and his overall contributions to the relationship with Jen. For every vice within us there is also a virtue, said Abraham Lincoln. Rick might have been a fighter– righteous and determined. He might have been willing to sacrifice and compromise everything for her. Rick might have done all that he could to provide for Jen and make her happy. It is impossible for us to esteem ourselves if we fail to recognize and appreciate our own strengths, endlessly lambaste ourselves or glorify others at our own expense, and if you are coming out of an abusive or otherwise unhealthy situation, then you are undoubtedly going to be left with a barrage of emotional wounds (The Patterns of Codependency).

In addition to examining self-esteem and the need for perfection, it is the role of this chapter to replace self-directed and self-destructive, misconceived, negative assumptions and projections regarding yourself and your part in the relationship with a rational and positive outlook, and in conjunction with the proceeding section, to replace erroneous self-conceived impressions about your former mate and the relationship with realistic notions.

Do not be shocked. Your relationship, as well as your conclusion as to why it ended, was a projection or assumption based on *your* reasoning, *your* rationale and *your* expectations. You cannot read another's mind, and through retrospect, you may soon discover that you were two people who were separated by different agendas.

CHAPTER III: Be Thankful

"I just don't know how I am going to continue on without her!" Love carries the narcotic effect of rendering us incoherent to the undesirable behaviors of the "gods" and "goddesses" who abandon us. As a result, we deify the one who deserted us, often at the expense of our self-esteem, and romanticize the relationship that we *thought* we had. We long for a false image of whom and what we lost–an illusion–rather than make a clear and rational judgment that the "prodigal" son or daughter for whose return we yearn for so desperately may not merit the naïve and disproportionate adoration and idolization that we attribute to them. Their erratic and questionable behaviors are often obvious to the rest of the world, however, which is why we hear friends and family remark, "What did you see in him?" You might have chosen to lay a blind eye to their emotional or physical treatment rather than confront the harsh reality of what they were doing (Loftus). Their intentions might have been masked by layers of deception. Therefore, *distorted memory, applied selective memory reprogramming* and *re-association* are addressed in this chapter, along with continued application of Freudian perspectives that account for our compulsion to seek harmful people and circumstances.

Much of the depression that afflicts us during the aftermath of abandonment is actually erroneous inwardly misdirected anger and blame. This deadly, self-induced and self-directed burden must be shifted away from ourselves and redirected toward its appropriate recipients if we are to begin to recover. Replacing idealistic and inaccurate perceptions of your former partner(s) and the relationship that you thought you had with more realistic and rational ones will relieve you of the destructive negative self-rapport and detestable image that you have sculpted for yourself (Memory).

Here my poor Bridget's corpse doth lie, she is at rest,-and so am I.

Poor Richard's Almanack

Directly attributable to our nature and backgrounds is our apparent inclination toward pessimistic thinking (Messina). Frequently we are unaware of the silver lining which accompanies that dark, frightening cumulonimbus cloud that has wrought its wrath with its mighty storm. We choose to see the metaphorical glass of water as half empty rather than half full. Prolonged unhealthy exposure to Jen, for example, undoubtedly would have wreaked havoc on Rick's confidence and prevented him from meeting someone more desirable and better suited for him. Do not be afraid of new people and new experiences. You need not fear the unknown and untried. Look ahead with wonder and enthusiasm to the road not taken.

CHAPTER IV: Reach Out-You Are Not Alone

Jack's queen played a deadly game of Blind Man's Bluff, feigning interest in a Vegas marriage, assuming that he would cash in his chips. She was a smooth dealer. When he anted and shocked his queen with a diamond, then she folded and broke his heart, telling him that he was not playing with a full deck.

Gerry carried on with another woman for three years unsuspectingly while misleading Jenny for eight, believing that they would be married when the time was "right."

Lenny up and left his wife and three children after ten years for a girl who was old enough to be his son's prom date.

Sabrina ruthlessly dropped her avid admirer after he had served his purpose of helping her mend her own broken heart from a previous failed relationship.

Marjorie could no longer compete with the sweet sixteen-year-olds whom her husband was entertaining or could Sandra, whose husband wanted a wife and child all in one.

In the midst of his pain and devastation, Deborah stared at Mike, completely devoid of emotion and compassion, and told him that there was another man in her life. In the end, she acted as if they had never even met.

Sandy seemed to enjoy torturing Kerry, knowing that what she was doing was wrong.

Sid is one of the kindest persons whom a woman could ask for, so why is his wife suing for divorce and child support after abusing and cheating on him throughout their marriage?

Drew continued to mislead Tristan into believing that they had a future together, having long made the decision to cast her out of his life when somebody new entered the scene.

It happens to men and women every day and right out of the blue. "I want a divorce." "This relationship isn't working out." "I don't love you anymore!" You are doubtlessly experiencing feelings and thinking thoughts that you would never have thought imaginable, but as alone as you may be feeling right now in your situation and in your devastation, you are among a considerable number of other men and women suffering similar circumstances and identical feelings. Depression, pain, fear, anger, guilt, shame, suicidal thoughts–these are expected following the aftermath of a separation and are not at all uncommon. The extent to which one experiences several or more of these thoughts and feelings may vary, of course, depending on the circumstances surrounding the breakup and your degree of sensitivity. Some abandonment victims recover within a year while for others, three to five years or longer may pass before they can live a life liberated from most of these symptoms, but above all, regardless of the extent to which you are suffering right now, the feelings shall subside with time, and a crucial factor in lessening your pain and quickening your recovery is the knowledge that you are not alone in your situation or your feelings, as drastic and as devastating as they may be right now.

Friends, support groups, therapists–here the immeasurable benefit of commiserating is addressed and encouraged but only with empathetic and supportive sources. "Oh, but I don't want to be a burden!" You will be more of a burden if they have to attend your funeral, and if they really do find helping you to be an encumbrance, then it is high time that you examined the friends and acquaintances in your

It is better to go to the house of mourning than to go to the house of feasting.
ECCLESIASTES 7:2

life as well as the partners that you choose for yourself. In all likelihood you will find similarities among all. The knowledge that your situation or suffering is not unique will take off some of the edge. Misery loves company, and one truth of importance that will support you through this time is listening to others with similar or even more devastating tales. Likewise, it is equally important for you to share your own story as well as your thoughts and feelings. You need to be heard as well as to hear. Commiseration is a vital component of the healing process, and it is of mutual support. It can be extremely liberating and enlightening. By talking to others, you release a great deal of your pain, and it also exposes you to newer perspectives. They in turn are benefited by yours. We are usually unable to see beyond our own often distorted assumptions and conclusions. Objective and outside ears can indeed be a life saver. You will discover, to your relief, that you were not the only one who was deceived, used, abused and abandoned. Your own feelings of devastation will be mitigated as you share your story and listen to the nightmarish tales told by others. Be on your guard, however, and remember to take with a grain of salt the words and comments of those who have not undergone a heart trauma. They may not be very patient, sympathetic or understanding; indeed, their words can even be detrimental. The truth is that nobody can fully empathize with the excruciating pain of heartbreak until it has happened to them. Do not buy into any derogatory remarks regarding your sensitivity or emotional well-being by friends and family who are unable or unwilling to bear with you during this difficult time. Your capacity for love and pain is actually testimony to your wholeness as a human being, and as dreadful as you may feel right now, you are in fact more fortunate than those who appear to deny their pain effectively. You will see this for yourself eventually. Do not heed the antiquated norms about masculinity and femininity. Indeed, it is these distorted values that stigmatize men especially into withholding emotions from others, further magnifying the pain. Stories involving other people in a wide variety of similar circumstances are included. You are not alone. What you are feeling is normal and natural. If you are encountering friends and family who are telling you to "Get over it already!" then again, you might want to evaluate the people in your life, and consider a change with whom you choose to acquaint yourself. You have every reason and every right to feel distraught. Through support groups, you will encounter many sensitive, empathetic and understanding people who are going through similar experiences.

CHAPTER V: Forgive-And Forget

"Forgive him? I'll never forget this for as long as I live!" *Put on then compassion, kindness, lowliness, meekness and patience, forbearing one another and, if one has a complaint against another, forgiving each other* (Cl. 3:12-13). Your boyfriend's or girlfriend's actions may have concealed a world of pain, confusion, fear and insecurity, and what we interpret as callousness may sometimes be nothing more than sheer ignorance and crudeness. Awareness of this perspective may lighten some of the sting resulting from a self-absorbed perception of fault and inadequacy, making forgiveness more tolerable. Psychologist Chuck Gallozzi likened the hidden psychological injuries of unfriendly and unhappy people to those of an injured and disfigured stray that bit his befriended master, having had escaped a brutal attack by some unknown person(s). The next time that you feel hurt by someone, he advised, pause and imagine this traumatized animal (Psychic Journal).

While a life of success may indeed be a positive and tangible reply toward one who has injured you, it is an attitude of forgiveness that is the sweetest revenge and certainly the simplest and sweetest remedy for a wounded heart. Simple does not always mean easy, of course, for forgiveness, as any other virtue, takes commitment and practice. Love and forgiveness are not only guidelines from the sages and prophets of the ages but attitudes that promote a happier and healthier life. Release the internal resentment and hostility that you harbor toward your former mate. The spiritual path is a challenging one that requires our effort from one moment to the next (Lozoff). It contradicts all of our die-hard values of strength, tenacity, honor, pride, justice, fairness and selfishness, but the payoff is immense, as we see in the peaceful demeanor of the Dalai Lama, the serenity of the Buddha and the countenance of all of the saints and prophets of the ages. Practice makes perfect, and it is that first step along the path that is always the hardest.

Bob's ex-wife is having second thoughts about the abusive man for whom she left him and their child and hints at coming back. It did not take long for Alan to find a woman to appreciate him after being left by his wife who even now, fifteen years later, cannot seem to find another man who treated her as nicely as he did. You need not punish or wish ill will toward your former partner or anyone else who has wronged you, however, for this only intensifies and prolongs your own suffering. Conversely, some compassion and forgiveness would be tenfold in speeding your path to recovery. Like the IRS, which has to funnel through mounds of tax returns but gets to yours eventually, time and conscience get around to everyone ultimately.

Learning to forgive is challenging. We must attempt to resolve the mind's compulsion to repeat past traumatic experiences and rectify unresolved hostilities and resentments through absolution for all those whom we determined have persecuted us, those who have abandoned us, first and foremost. This, in addition to resolving control issues, will help release or alleviate the tenacious hold that our former partners and associated experiences and expectations have.

Forget. As a child can repeatedly leave behind even his most prized possessions the moment he is distracted by something else compelling and exciting, so does the *interference theory* (Loftus) address the element of time and applied psychology for erasure of memories and associations (Merriam-Webster; World Book Online).

CHAPTER VI: Let Time Heal

"Put it behind you," they nonchalantly suggest as if you had not already considered that option for yourself. The impact is real. You cannot deny this reality any more than you can deny having a broken arm. Do not expect success overnight, however, regardless of the pressures put upon you by yourself and others. Recovery takes time. Expect to find a pot of gold at the end of a rainbow, and you shall surely be disappointed. Gather one talent at a time; however, look behind you, and you shall truly see the wealth of progress that you have made on your road to recovery and self-discovery. But know that it is forthcoming. Genuine happiness comes from hard work and accomplishment. Trial, error and struggle result in knowledge and wisdom. Practice makes perfect. If all of our experiences in life were only smooth and blissful, then we would not achieve greatness. We would never have the opportunity to learn or develop as individuals. Your first step, diploma, degree, license and move were difficult. You may not remember the hard work, striving, fear and uncertainty, but you did experience these challenges to some extent and grew wiser, stronger and better from them. You overcame hurdles and attained heights that you never would have reached had you not suffered trials and tribulation. *It's not the top; it's the climb* (Lozoff).

It may take a while, but let time heal itself. Time; friends; family; therapy; change; faith; activity; passions; plans; self-respect; self-awareness; depersonalizing; surrender and yes, forgiveness, will get you through this difficult time. Enjoy life. Make money. Spend money. Comfort yourself. Treat yourself to that trip to Europe. Trade in your jalopy for that brand new car on which you have had your eyes for so long. Go on a shopping spree at Macy's and Bloomingdale's. Make a change in your wardrobe (you may not have much of a choice now that your waist has probably been altered by two inches). Drink from fine crystal, and dine on expensive china. Enjoy a sumptuous dinner at Tavern on the Green or another of those exquisite restaurants that you never felt you deserved to patronize. We shell out hundreds each month for rent, mortgage, bills and traffic tickets.

You have heard it said before that time heals all wounds. Ask those who have suffered a loss similar to yours, and they will all tell you the same thing—"It took a while, but I got over it." According to Dr. Paul Pearsall's Law of Impermanence, *everything changes and nothing ever stays the same. Where there is sadness and sorrow, happiness is waiting right around the corner.* This will happen gradually and methodically, but it shall happen. *The Holy Scriptures* guarantee it. *How much greener are the pastures in the wake of a storm?* Look ahead, but be reasonable in your projections, and do not expect immediate results. True, you may experience some intermittent moments of relief, but these momentary highs are usually followed by lows of equal intensity as you trek through the recovery process. Give yourself a three- to five-year perspective (Brown). Know that you will enjoy being alive again by then, and if you get over it sooner, then consider yourself very fortunate. In the meantime, the adventure is just beginning, and a better life lies ahead.

The Grand essentials of happiness are
something to do,
something to love,
and something to hope for.
Allan K. Chalmers

A time to weep, and a time to laugh
ECCLESIASTES 3:3

The universe grants us
that which we seek.

CHAPTER I
Take Responsibility

CHAPTER I: Take Responsibility

Here's to those who love not wisely.
Frank Sinatra

Your Track Record

You always want what you cannot have, your mother lectures. "Lydia was crazy about you!" "She would have done anything to make you happy!" mom adds. "What is with you and these older men?" dad wants to know. "I am going to have a son-in-law my own age who calls me dad!" he banters on. "The man should be older and wiser than the woman," preached grandpa with his age-old wisdom. "And why can't you meet someone nice for once?" "She never looks me in the face." "They say that a person who doesn't like animals..." "Dogs, cats and little children always know!" "If he treats his own mother that way..." "The apple doesn't fall far from the tree." "The man is supposed to be the breadwinner of the family!" "Birds of a feather..." "If he's like that now..." "Do not believe everything you hear." "Beauty is only skin deep." "If he does not call you the next day to say thanks..." "If she will not open the lock on your side..." "A guy over twenty-five still living at home with his parents..." "A gentleman always opens the door for the lady." You do not want to admit it, but deep inside you know that your parents are right.

Many complain of their memory, few of their judgment, spoke Benjamin Franklin in the early eighteenth century. Perhaps Poor Rich was right. Many of us habitually make poor choices in men and women or in friends and acquaintances overall. If you reflect on your past relationships, then you may very well discover that the men or women in your life were similar to the person with whom you were recently involved. You may notice a pattern (Staton). It is time for self-honesty. You may be consciously or unconsciously asking the universe for the type of man or woman that you are meeting, and you are only receiving what you ordered. Likewise, you are what they are seeking, so do not be so surprised when they surprise you. We witness men and women endlessly complaining about their partners' abuse and deception only to find an identical successor once they leave or have been abandoned. Battered women perpetually meet battering men. We grow frustrated watching our friends and loved ones get involved with the same people and the same insanity over and over again. "And they could have had someone nice, like me!"

You resented your parents' meddling in your affairs. You thought that mom was being old-fashioned when she implored you to stick to somebody like yourself. Dad was protecting you when he insisted on meeting those brutes who were double parked and honking their horns outside while you were reaching for your coat, purse and hurrying out the door. There is a reason why the father traditionally granted permission for his daughter's hand in marriage. Even your grandparents had something to say, but you were indignant and told them to stay out of it. You did not heed their wisdom and advice. You rebelled.

Rose-colored Glasses

"How could they do this to me?" you continue to cry out in disbelief. "We had such a wonderful thing together!" "I'll never find anybody like her again!" "He was the perfect man!" "We were meant to be together!" You miss her. Of course you do. The grass is always greener on the other side. Who would not miss the perfect relationship with the perfect person? You ruminate incessantly. You fixate on the smiles, the wonderful times that you shared together, her cute looks, his sweet personality and her tender voice. Perhaps Sally laughed at everything that you said because, as Benjamin Franklin would say, she enjoyed flaunting her fine teeth. Maybe Mark enjoyed those "wonderful times together" for selfish reasons unbeknown to Pat. Terry's agenda and motives might have been different from those of Drew's completely.

You want to know how your "partner" could "flat leave" you. You are shocked, confused, hurt. It was going to be a marriage made in

Heaven. *Grace is deceitful, and beauty is in vain* (Pr. 31:30), and if you examine the "relationship" in retrospect carefully, then you are likely to discover a host of warning signs that you failed to see–or did not want to see–from early on during your time together. These clues are often subtle and combined with positive gestures, resulting in mixed messages as well as misleading ones.

You Asked for It

Did you meet a nice girl as your mother wanted you to, or were they mean, arrogant, pretentious, selfish and spoiled? You did not listen to her when she said that she smelled a rat, that there was just something not right about him; you had to find out the hard way. Dad did not like John, and mom never trusted Mai. "What does an older lady want with my son," she mulled, and why did she always get her way?" "Your new boyfriend never comes inside to meet me," dad ponders with misgivings. Little did he know that Tommy was twice your age, that David hit you and that Glen was married. "And Lydia was so sweet!" mom mused. You emphatically said, "No thank you!" when your aunt said that she had a nice boy in mind. Maybe you preferred the "bad boys" who showed up an hour late half the time. "Don't you go chasing that girl!" mom said sternly. "Let them chase after you," dad advised. "Why is she fifty-four and still not married?" your parents wondered. "She is very unusual!" your friends tried to hint to you as tactfully as they could. "Why did three wives decide to leave?" they all questioned with suspicion. Let's face it; even you had your doubts.

This does not mean to imply that you were to blame for the termination of the relationship, and it certainly does not suggest that the other person's behavior was justified, but it does hold you accountable for repeated mismatches, extended exposure to ill treatment and for allowing that final act of insult and injury when you should have had the good sense and judgment to abandon them first after the initial signs of trouble.

X Red Flags X

"You can do better than me." "Maybe you should date others!" The sweet, unspoiled girl who once told you that she wanted a simple house wedding suddenly insists that the reception be held at the Waldorf Astoria. "Promise me that you'll never leave me!" she cries. Now she is the one leaving you.

People sometimes speak of omens–small and isolated signs that exemplify and foretell patterns of greater intensity later on. Teachers, for example, can identify children who will ceaselessly vie in a year-long power struggle from the onset of a new school year. We know that first impressions are often indicative of a person's general attitudes, behavior and overall personality.

Actions Speak Louder Than Words

She gave you more impossible and unreasonable demands than Austria gave Serbia right before World War I and blamed you for the fall of the Roman Empire. She had been pushing marriage suddenly even though she had once told you that marriage was not for her. Now she *wants* a baby even though she is fifty-three and a year into menopause. Your first big fight was over Johnny Mathis, who became the "other man." "Guess we're just not compatible," she justified. She rejected every hall and house that you liked after asking your opinion first.

He went from praises to putdowns, from Godiva to Nestles. The flowers and the flattery wilted after the first month. You eagerly cooked for him. He found cooking for you a chore. You made love; she had sex–she found that a chore, too.

He gave you every reason in the book why a relationship with him would not work.

She made you feel like an inconvenience, in the way and a burden on her time and space.

You were granted just a little too much freedom.

He never insisted that you telephone him after you had arrived home safely.

Carrie's Christmas gift from Jamie after ten years was a gift certificate. Gerry surprised Ronnie with a wig for Valentines Day. Ally's husband would not even get her a card for her birthday. Lou has them all beat. He took his wife out to dinner for her special day and gave her the check.

"Hurt me once, shame on you, but hurt me twice…" Previous breakups by the same person or suggestions that the two of you see other people or say anything else discouraging are sure signs of a relationship's impending destine. You might have chosen to remain oblivious to these and other subtle innuendos that you were never a priority in his or her life to begin with, and its termination was simply a matter of time.

He who loves you will share with you the bad times as well as the good. She who cares will always be there for you when the going gets rough. A true relationship withstands the test of misfortune.

Perhaps he tried to get you angry at him, hoping that you would break it off first. In Elaine May's 1972 film *The Heartbreak Kid*, Lenny provokes an altercation with the waiter to frighten off his newly wedded Lila. When he realizes that his attempts are futile, then he has to finally confront her and tell her the truth. Petty arguments and fault-finding are signs of sabotage and not a personal reflection on you. You might have been railroaded out of the relationship.

Every action has an equal and opposite reaction. Easy come, easy go. Relationships that begin intensely and passionately usually end just as quickly and suddenly. Successful relationships are cultivated. They need time to nurture and grow.

Perhaps your nephew or niece expressed her opinion. Children are good judges of character, and like radar, they can spot insincerity and superficiality a mile away.

Consider the way that she treated her children from her other marriage. A parent who put you before her own children will subsequently put others before you.

Did your cat come down to greet him or hiss at him? Did your dog go for his throat? Like children, animals have an intuitive sense and can readily detect fear, discomfort and people with abrasive natures. How a person reacts to pets is also an indication of their disposition. If they could be cruel to animals, then they could be cruel to you, too. If they could abandon a former pet, then they could abandon you as well.

Very often friends and family will be alerted to ominous clues, actions and behaviors long before you are. In *The Heartbreak Kid*, Kelly's father is opposed to his daughter's engagement to Lenny, reproving of his shallow career, his infidelity toward his newly wedded wife in favor of Kelly, his blatant attempts to impress their family with guile and insincerity and his overall personality, referring to him as a "nut." Love blinded Mike to the bizarre idiosyncrasies of his former fiancée, but they were clear as day to the world around him.

At this point, you may be asking, "Well, if he were not interested, then why would he have stayed with me for as long as he did?" Step outside of your own thinking, logic, values and motives. Others are not necessarily motivated by the same interests as we are. Through projection, we attribute our own assumptions onto the world us. Maybe he did not look forward to that trip to Bermuda with the same excitement as you. Perhaps she did not share in your pleasures and show an equal amount of interest in the outings and activities that were appealing to you. Assumptions are part of what blinded us to the reality that our former partners may not have been the saints that we thought they were or that our marriage or relationship was not in fact made in Heaven. Similarly, they might have chosen not to remain with you for the length of time that they did for factors alien to your own reasoning. *Their lips drop honey and their mouth is smoother than oil, but in the end they are bitter as wormwood* (Pr. 5:3-4). If you are not a user, for example, then you might not readily fathom that your former companion might have enjoyed the free dinners, the all-expense-paid vacations, the presents, the favors, the scholarship, the ego boost you provided for them, especially around their friends and colleagues, the sex and the gaps that you filled until something of "greater value" came along. None of these aforementioned benefits necessitated or presupposed any emotional attachment to you. *They that seek my hurt meditate deceits all the day long* (Ps. 38:12). You might have simply played the roles of dinner host, travel guide, Santa Claus, playboy centerfold or GQ. If your generosity was exploited, then they may not even have stayed with you for as long as they did had you asked that they split the dinner check with you earlier on during the relationship. Marie, for example, nearly spit out her after-dinner drink when the man whom she was dating asked her to help pay the tab for the first time. Every dark cloud has a silver lining; though, so even if you were simply a temporary time filler or place holder, the mere fact that they even chose to be around you for that period of time negates any assumptions that you were the diabolical villain responsible for the demise of the relationship even if they claimed you were. It is better to have loved and lost. It is a compliment in disguise and flattering that they would want to spend time with you and share the same bed with you in the first place, and remember, if the former man or woman in your life was motivated by insincerity and ill intentions, then naturally they are going to make you the scapegoat for their taking leave of you. Most people would just as soon pass the blame onto others rather than accept responsibility for the harm that they bring. This repressed accountability, however, festers deep inside of the human psyche and may poison it in the form of unresolved guilt and shame (Messina). People who dismiss their thoughts and deny their feelings tend to inflict themselves with obsessive and destructive behavior as they continue to live a deluded life devoid of reality. They live life in an endless destructive pattern, misleading others, hurting them and denying the pain and suffering that they cause, rationalizing their actions through self-righteousness, judgment and blame.

Just as we are blinded by our assumptions, we are also blinded by our egos, and by understanding that everyone with whom we share a relationship may not actually love us, you can considerably reduce and work toward eliminating the shock of the other's unfazed ability to take their leave of you after all that you "shared." This is an especially vile awakening for the innocent, naïve and first time lover who may have experienced love loss for the first time, and this ravaging blow can strike anybody at any age.

> I have always thought the actions of
> men the best interpreters of their thoughts.
> John Locke

A Lamb stood drinking early one morning on the bank of a woodland stream. That very same morning a hungry Wolf came by farther up the stream, hunting for something to eat. He soon got his eyes on the Lamb. As a rule Mr. Wolf snapped up such delicious morsels without making any bones about it, but this Lamb looked so very helpless and innocent. "How dare you paddle around in my stream and stir up all the mud!" he shouted fiercely. "You deserve to be punished severely for your rashness!" "But, your highness," replied the trembling Lamb, "I cannot possibly muddy the water you are drinking up there. You are upstream and I am down stream." "I have heard that you told lies about me last year!" "How could I have done so?" pleaded the Lamb. "I wasn't born until this ear." "Well, then it was someone in your family, but no matter who it was, I do not intend to be talked out of my breakfast."

An Aesop Fable

Other Early Warning Signs

- *Avoids your family and friends*

- *Stingy*

- *Disrespectful toward you, your family and friends*

- *Critical & judgmental*

- *Not eager to make an impression on your family and friends*

- *Doesn't display courtesy such as opening the lock on the driver's side, calling a cab, opening the door for you, ringing your bell or seeing you to your door*

- *Frequent lateness, postpones or cancels dates*

- *Rarely compliments*

- *History of multiple & short-lived relationships*

- *Places unusual and unfair demands*

- *Always busy*

- *Telephones infrequently*

- *Flirtatious*

- *Always anxious to part company with you*

Additional Warning Signs

- *Makes frequent excuses*

- *Evades talk of marriage*

- *Unforgiving*

- *Places time restrictions*

- *Uncompromising*

- *Unsupportive*

- *Fosters jealousy & insecurity*

- *Secretive*

- *Easily annoyed*

- *Prefers to be with friends*

- *Displays little affection*

- *Unfaithful*

- *Intolerant*

- *Minimizes birthdays & other occasions*

- *Abusive*

A Marriage Made in Heaven

When I was younger I could remember anything, whether it had happened or not, wrote Mark Twain. It is baffling how we are left with such a utopian image of those who hurt us. We forget their unpleasant characteristics, actions and behaviors while it is difficult to recall the negative experiences that we had during the relationship. Benjamin Franklin said that creditors have better memories than debtors. *Memory feeds imagination,* notes Amy Tan, and naturally we overlook and forget people, places and events that bring us emotional pain and discomfort (Memory). We often forget, procrastinate or choose not to confront a supervisor, pay a fine, our debts and begin work on that big project. It should not come as a mystery that we choose to repress and deny unwanted signs that the man or woman whom we adore does not feel likewise. Our psyche, judgment and intuition are extremely sensitive and sharp. Your instincts might have sensed that something was questionable right from the very beginning, and they forewarned you. You did not want to believe or accept your hunches, however, and you avoided confronting the truth for as long as you could. This is not to say that the other party was not to blame for misleading you or not being straight with you; of course, they might have been confused themselves, but had you heeded the weather forecast before you set sail on this perilous journey and jumped ship at the first sight of the imminent storm, then you would have steered clear of the turbulent waters in which you now find yourself submerged.

By *repression* and a*voidance,* not only do we spurn our sixth sense, but we contaminate our thoughts and emotions as well (Loftus). It is no wonder why we are continually bombarded with triggering reminders, feel guilty about everything that we did or failed to do and take the blame for their actions and folly. We live a lie, in a perpetual hallucinatory state. With the aid of a therapist, friends and family who knew your lover and through retrospective reflection, we can recall and bring to surface many of those early warning signs and begin to dissociate and dispel much of the erroneous perception that we hold for our dream lovers and wake ourselves up from this nightmare. Recall those early premonitions. Scan your memory for those brazen remarks, her sadistic treatment, his bullying, her threats, the lies and the lame excuses. Recall how it felt not being included on her list of priorities, when he was just too busy to see you more often. You strengthen your memory as you strengthen your muscles–through repetition. Ruminate about *these* things until the fictitious character whom only you have created is destroyed.

Repression plays a prevalent part in deluding us with exaggerated notions and false memories. Richard Webster illustrates this with a story about Freud, who as a little boy, erroneously "remembered" seeing his mother naked when in fact it was later determined that this never actually took place. Freud's delusive memory may have actually been a manifestation of the *Oedipus complex.* In wanting to possess his mother, Freud's mind may have been inclined toward such a wish. Wishful thinking or false memory was the central theme in John Brabourne's and Richard B. Goodwin's theatrical release *A Passage to India,* in which Adela Quested, having had fantasies about being forced into sex, is self-deluded into believing that Dr. Aziz had raped her. The film shows the accused facing a trial on a false allegation of sexual assault, similar to the occasional false claims of girls in schools who spin yarns about sexual misconduct from male teachers. Ninety-five percent of the time these men are about as guilty as the nineteen witches in 1692 Salem. Even renowned researcher in psychology John Henry Wigmore warned of women and girls being predisposed to bringing accusations against men of good character (Webster). Through *selective memory*, we disregard or overlook intransitive senses intentionally (Baker). We cease to remember or notice that which we do not wish to acknowledge. We see what we want to see, and then we want to know how this person could suddenly change. But he has not changed. She is no different than she was from the onset. We were simply living a protective state of denial and were thus blinded to reality.

The past is malleable and flexible, says Peter Berger, changing as our recollection interprets and re-explains what has happened (Brainy Media). It usually takes others to remind you of how unhappy you were when you were "happily" employed.

Forgetting is part of memory's normal operation. Imagine how awful it would be to remember every hurt feeling and every unpleasant experience (Loftus). Through *memory filtering,* we unconsciously tamper with the memory, leaving some things out, for example, or adding a detail that seems relevant at the moment. Through your own denial of the harsh reality of your former partner and former relationship, you may have tuned out many unpleasant thoughts, memories and feelings, longing for and perpetuating a glorified version of both; thus, you cannot trust your memory, for it is full of distortions, exaggerations and delusions. We usually do not vividly remember other people and events the way that they actually were. Our memories cannot be fully trusted. They are not always accurate, and more often they are not always objective (World Book). Mike yearns for those wonderful trips that he took with Leila for which she always seemed to struggle to make time. He misses holding her in his arm while she looked at the watch on hers. Cameron envisions Morgan spending time with her niece but not the arguments or the critical remarks made about her father. Dee laments over Michelle's words of wisdom instead of recalling her statements of ignorance.

What Is This Thing Called Love?

This is a term that is about as sacred as the word "married" and spoken almost as often as the word "got." Many people use this term with their partners in much the same context as one would "love" to look at the wedding, baby or vacation photos of their friends and colleagues. People seem to have more love for their first cup of coffee in the morning than they do for their lovers. I cringe every time that I pass an attorney's window front that reads: "Divorce! Only $500.00! Quick and Easy!" It is unfortunate that so many people go through life with perpetual misconceptions regarding love and marriage. They expect to see fireworks or feel a permanent sense of satisfaction and fulfillment, and when either is lacking, it is onto the next. After delivering a tribute to her sister on her wedding day recently, a colleague was asked by one of the guests what had held her parents together for over forty years. She replied to the gentleman at the table with a simple two-word response: Love endures.

Love desires you. It knows you well and is fond of you. It is attached to you by affection and esteem. Love respects and thinks highly of you. It admires, adores and idolizes you. It has no aversion toward you or repulsion. It does not look upon you with disgust or contempt. It does not look down upon you with disfavor or scorn. It does not harbor resentment, or does it denounce or condemn. It neither has personal enmity, nor does it oppose you on principle. It loves you for who you are. It neither minds who you are, nor does it matter (Webster's New World Dictionary and Thesaurus 2: 209+; Miriam-Webster Collegiate Dictionary 11: 413+).

Love is truthful. Love neither deceives nor misleads, nor does it betray or deny you. Love is loyal, faithful and honorable. It keeps its word (*Holy Bible* 1007).

Love does not abuse you. It does not humiliate you. Love does not hurt. Love with conditions is not love. Love does not threaten or give ultimatums. It does not keep you guessing, wondering or worrying. It does not have you walking on eggshells or thin ice. It neither is hostile, antagonistic nor seeks to injure or confound (*Holy Bible* 1007).

Love puts you first. It makes time for you. It is never too busy. Love sacrifices. It puts its own needs aside. Love is responsive (*New World Translation of the Holy Scriptures* 1435).

Love sympathizes. It is an ally, a supporter and a friend. It waits with you and stays by your side. It never gives up hope (*Holy Bible* 1007). It does not avoid you or desert you in your time of trouble. It shares your fortunes and misfortunes. It listens to your deepest dark secrets without judgment. Love cares. Love is concerned. It defends and protects you. Love laughs and cries with you.

Love is intimate, close and bonding. It is dear, kind, helpful and well-disposed. Love is warmhearted, tenderhearted, sentimental, emotional, well-intentioned, attentive and companionable (*New*

World Translation of the Holy Scriptures 1435).

Love forgives. It is an act of endless forgiveness; thus, if they could not forgive you, then they could not have loved you. Love tolerates. It does not renounce, blame, scold or rebuke. Love welcomes you. It appreciates and cherishes you (*Holy Bible* 1007).

Love is friendship and friendship is love (Miriam-Webster); if one ceases, then the other never existed.

Love endures hardships. It is devoted and dedicated. It grows stronger with time, not weaker. It neither tires of you, nor does it reject you. It continues to grow even over the longest distances. *A wife should not depart from her husband and a husband should not leave his wife.* (1 Co. 7:10-11) Love is forever (*Holy Bible* 1007).

You loved your parents. You may not have necessarily liked everything about them, and you might have been repeatedly annoyed by their attitude and behavior at times, but except in exceptionally rare cases you would never abandon your parents. They quarreled with each other. They bickered with you. Still, despite these annoyances and hardships, you could never even imagine life without them. Infatuation may disappear overnight but not love.

Too many people use the "L" word prematurely and frivolously. Countless couples marry much too soon because they *thought* that they loved each other. Being "in love" is being infatuated or obsessed, much as children in puppy love. Looking back, the relationship was probably not all that you remember it to be. When you are in love, you are living a fantasy. You are in love with what you *think* and *hope* that the other person is and what you think and hope that your relationship is. How many times do you hear people say, "This is definitely the one"–for the fifth time? "It was love at first sight." How can it be love at first sight when you hardly know them? These are the hopeless romantics who are in their fifties and still micro-waving their own dinners. Love comes after the honeymoon.

When you are in love, you may not in fact love the person himself but what he does for you. You love having, as Dr. Paul Pearsall put it, *someone who meets your own selfish needs as expressed by the brain's evolutionary directive for self-advancement* (177). Unfortunately, once these needs are fulfilled, one partner discovers quite suddenly that they really do not love you after all; hence, you are no longer needed or wanted. The man or woman who just could not wait to marry you now wants to divorce you. When you love a person, then you do so unconditionally, in sickness and in health, in good times and in bad. Some people are incapable of love. Any man or woman who can threaten the other with divorce or separation if they do not get their "act together" is revealing conditional love, a selfish, self-aggrandizing need to control, dominate and manipulate, and not a genuine love and concern for the person himself.

Absence makes the heart grow fonder, not farther. One who truly loves you will want to spend time with you and not away from you. Of course we all need our own personal time and space to one extent or another, but if he really wants to be with you, then he will do so. She will put aside most other priorities and not skip a weekend with you because she "saw too much of you" during the previous two weekends. He will call you just to say hello. She will welcome your calls at most any time of the day or night. You will not be a burden to see but a pleasure. Turn it around. He might not have been as eager about seeing you as you were about seeing him. Love is not proven by mere lip service but by deed. She will often go out of her way to cook for you. She will care for you. He will show concern and worry about your happiness and welfare even to the extent of putting himself in harm's way for you as you would for him. She is supportive, always having your best interests at heart. You would never have done to her what she did to you. It is doubtful that you would have abandoned him at the drop of a hat or in her hour of need, hurt her, held a grudge, threatened, humiliated, insulted or offended him. You would not have replaced him, allowed her to suffer or watched him cry. You would not have cast this person out of your life and into the world apart from you, never to be seen or heard from again without care or concern.

Pride and Prejudice
A Wrongdoer Is *Never* Recognized in His Own Home

Because you are not what I would have you be, I blind myself to what in truth you are, said Madeline L' Engle. We hear other people's stories and incredible tales of mayhem, mystery and disbelief. "Nobody I know!" you arrogantly conclude. "It could never happen to me!" "I know my men and women." Consider the long list of other characters with whom you had found yourself to this "exception to them all." We perceive what we project, and what we project is what we want to *believe*, what we *want* to see and what we are *prepared* to see.

Perhaps you remember the *Young Girl/Old Woman Illusion* from one of your high school or college classes (Weisstein). Akin to David Rumelhart's *schema theory,* the *top-down, bottom-up* theory of reading comprehension (Roswell and Natchez 144) explains that we often make word substitutions and omissions while reading because we bring our own life experience to the print (top-down) as well as reading what is actually printed (bottom-up), to wit, we see what we think we see, what we expect to see, what we hope to

To be in love is merely to be in a state of perceptual anesthesia-to mistake an ordinary young man for a Greek god or an ordinary young woman for a goddess.

H.L. Mencken

What we see depends mainly on what we look for.
Sir John Lubbock

see and what we want to see. Although objective and detached individuals may be the first to notice peculiarities and early warning signs, they are often uncomfortable about disclosing them to us until the relationship comes to a conclusion.

T /-\ E   C /-\ T

A look at the two middle letters above reveals that what we perceive actually depends in part on context and familiarity. Because of our extensive comprehensive experience with these words, for instance, we take for granted or assume the letters to be an H and an A when they are in fact neither (Buss 111-16). *Perceptual constancy* blinds us to reality, creates illusions and leads to assumptions and prejudice; thus, we are dumbfounded when people in whom we invest all of our trust and faith deceive us. They must have loved us, we presuppose; after all, we did share a relationship. How does one account for or justify children who abandon their elderly parents to nursing homes after they have been entrusted with their life savings? *Nothing is easier than self-deceit*, preached Demosthenes, *for what each man wishes is what he also believes to be true.*

Deception and betrayal are certainly not relegated to present times. Both have transpired repeatedly throughout the course of history: Marc Antony abandoned his wife for Cleopatra. He also conspired with Cleo against Octavian. Ptolemy murdered his wife because he had eyes for the daughter of the Greek king. Ptolemy XIII forced out his sister from the throne. Cain took the life of his brother. Adam and Eve betrayed God. Caesar neither suspected Brutus, nor did Washington suspect Arnold. Judas surprised the apostles.

Freudian psychology professes the concept of the *ego* and how the *libido* can direct narcissistic and idealistic images of ourselves toward our partners. This scientific analysis of love is enough to burst one's bubble, and it is this bubble that has left you bewildered in the wake of what has happened (Felluga). You have spawned, nurtured and fostered your own creation, an illusion, or as Goethe said, *the great majority loves in others only what they lend him, their own selves and their own version of him.* You have cast your own character, scripted your own storyline and have nominated them Best Actor or Best Actress of the Year in a widely acclaimed award winning Best Picture of the Year. Take responsibility for falling in love with your imagination.

By our fourth date, Hope had already had the song picked out for our wedding. She had the guest list drawn up, the hall reserved, the house built, the car started and the kids named. I was to be the groom, of course, the man of the hour. There was just one minor glitch-I didn't know about it.

Michael

Gods and Goddesses

Love is blind and lovers cannot see, according to William Shakespeare. When we are infatuated with another person, we can easily lose sight of the rational perspective that they too are human. They go to the bathroom, leave odors, wake up in the morning with foul breath and reek after a workout. They are not without failure, flaw, vice, resentment or prejudice, and they too have their qualms and idiosyncrasies. The loves of our lives can make moronic remarks and do ludicrous things, too. They are not divine and unblemished.

Was he there by your side when you were at your worst, or did he tell you to give him a call when things were looking up? We continue to idolize people who idolize themselves. We worship conceit, arrogance and callousness and squawk at kindness, sincerity and faithfulness. "If she's that interested in me, she must be desperate," we naively assume. "He must want something from me," we conclude. Our values are misplaced.

It is such a mysterious paradox how we are inclined to chase after and pine over people such as these and discount others who really do show fondness. Perhaps some of it is nothing more than pride. I was captive audience to a woman one evening who ranted about how much she could not stand the man with whom she lived and how desperately she wanted to break off her relationship with him, that was until she phoned home and heard the voice of another woman.

It is with what you are familiar, to what you are accustomed and the environment in which you have been reared. This does not require a Freudian researcher to understand. It is common knowledge. What you need to do, first of all, is recognize that for many years now, that you have probably been setting yourself up for rejection, doing yourself and others a disservice. The next thing that you obviously need to do is reverse this destructive pattern. I have actually heard people complain that the men or women in their lives loved them *too much*. I have witnessed some of the nicest people being abused and dropped out of their lovers' lives because they were too available, too sincere and unpretentious. Some were just "too nice." "Oh, what you see is what you get!" It is quite common for young adults to like the "bad boys" and "bad girls." If you truly want a permanent mate who in all likelihood will stay with you till death do you part, then you must allow them into your life instead of rejecting them for others who will eventually reject you after they have gotten all that they needed from you. But take some responsibility, and cease griping about the dwindling availability of good men and women out there whom you are making incessant excuses to pass up. It is your tendency to gravitate toward unavailable and abusive people and to turn away sincere and available people that has placed you in the situation that you are in right now, and unless you begin to accept loving, caring and available people into your life, then you are going to continue this cycle and bemoan your bad breaks and your solitude for years to come.

Perhaps she saw you at her convenience and when it benefited her, scheduling you last on her list of priorities. You should have expected a periodic call saying, "Hi, I was thinking about you." Chances are that he has not even reached out to you. Certainly you do not want someone who does not care or who is going to treat you disrespectfully.

"Where were you?" "Put on a jacket before you catch cold!" "I was worried about you!" If your "mate" failed to express worry with questions similar to these or make regular gestures of maternal or paternal love and concern, then in all probability they did not really care all that much about you in the first place. You may not have been a priority. It may not have mattered to them where you were, with whom you kept company or whether or not you were sick or injured. The mother who shakes and screams at her four-year-old for running into the street is displaying love and concern as opposed to the indifferent father who says, "Oh well, those are kids for you!" If your mate did not get upset with you for coming home late, failing to telephone her, neglecting your health and safety, traveling without him or "hanging out with the guys" too often, then the stake that he or she had in the relationship is highly questionable.

Commitment

"If only I met the right person," Kathleen pouts. "You are so fortunate to have a man like Mark," Jody enviously cries to her colleague. "Still together after twenty years," remarks a jealous Dannah to her coworker, "why can't *I* be that lucky?"

It is not luck, it is not the perfect man or woman (as if one actually existed), and it is not a marriage made in heaven, as these misinformed, unfortunate dreamers and other fifty-seven-year-old maids and butlers delude themselves into believing all of their lives. Relationships are difficult. Marriages are challenging. Things go wrong. Couples embrace each other one day and then fight with each other the next day. People are different. Successful partnerships require mutual tolerance, compromise and sacrifice. Nobody meets "The One." There is no "perfect man" or "perfect woman." All relationships fizzle after a brief honeymoon phase. Relationships and marriages sustain because two people have decided to honor their commitment to each other for better or for worse and because they understand what love and commitment are really all about. A commitment is a pledge, a guarantee, a duty, a promise and an obligation (Webster's New World Dictionary and Thesaurus 2: 122; Merriam-Webster Collegiate Dictionary 11: 250). It requires work and effort. Relationships also require periodic maintenance. Both partners need occasional stroking and reinforcement. In a relationship, one's own selfish needs and desires may be compromised for the love of his or her partner as well as for the benefit of the union itself (*Holy Bible* 668+). If he or she put herself first and failed to look out for your interests, then this was merely an arrangement, an affair, and not a relationship.

It is a travesty how once upon a time, nearly half of all divorcees stood before each other, the altar, the minister, God and witnesses, looked deep into each other's eyes and emphatically swore, "I do!" Except for extreme circumstances, one should not abandon his companion. The effects are internal, emotional and psychological. Unless one is without conscience, there is bound to be some remorse and regret for having torn a bond with somebody or having injured another person, for the conscience is not only God's rendezvous point with us but also His high court and prison.

Surely, as a faithless wife leaves her husband, so have you been faithless to me, says the Lord.

Jeremiah 3:20

A CRIME AGAINST GOD

God and state law have reasons why a relationship is binding. There is an explanation why getting a divorce is like pulling teeth or why it requires grounds and mutual consent. The Hawaiian culture believes that all relationships are permanent. We are all connected, and once you lose a person, you lose a part of yourself (Pearsall). Unfortunately, marriage vows are mere lip service to God and the state half of the time. Not everybody marries out of love for the other person. Some marry for financial security and others out of wedlock. Others choose mates out of loneliness. Some need a male to father their child. For others it is a show or an act of defiance.

People who love and care for the welfare of the other do not need the law to enforce a commitment, however, for God is the Supreme Magistrate over all relationships, and an act of betrayal against another is an act of betrayal against God. There are consequences for our actions, and like our local judicial system, they may not be immediate but forthcoming nonetheless. Could you sleep at night knowing that you hurt another?

Every relationship has trials and struggles. People who romantically delude themselves into believing that love is only bliss set themselves up for disappointment and relationship problems. They are blind to the true nature and challenges of loving. It is these dreamers who are still looking and will no doubt continue this perpetual delusion until they are sixty, seventy and beyond. It comes down to not so much as whether Tom is a better choice than Dick but whether or not Mary wants to be in a relationship or marriage. The divorce rate is higher now than it was in the thirties and forties even though husbands and wives had conflicts in those days as well.

Some people choose to remain in relationships after many years while others look back with regret. The former are those who know that no man or woman is without flaw and that no relationship is without blemish. They are able to recognize and appreciate the attributes of their partners instead of judging and focusing on the negative aspects of their natures. These are men and women who

I, (name), take you; (name), to be my (husband/wife).
I promise to be true to you in good times and in bad, in
sickness and in health. I will love you and honor you
all the days of my life.

Roman Catholic Wedding Vow

understand the difference between love and lust; love and infatuation
and reality versus fantasy. They appreciate coming home to someone, someone who loves and cares. Pauline and Nat have been
together for fifty-three years, a span that saw their friends and
relatives married two and three times. Paula and Randy are together
twenty-six years and still going strong. Next year will be Lisa's and
Scott's twentieth anniversary. All have chosen to remain with each
other because they appreciate the love and companionship.

From "I Do" to "I Don't"

Marisa was to be married. Arrangements were made and the hall
scheduled and paid for. A month prior to the big day, she discovered
that her groom had been seeing another woman. After three years
married to Joe, and all seemingly well, Lee learned that he had been
sleeping with other people. Tammy was sleeping with another man
the night before her wedding day with Mickey, whom she divorced
three years later. Mae was seeing several men all throughout her
engagement to her fiancé.

The divorce rate in our country for the newly wedded in 1997
was 50 percent with a 43 percent likelihood after 7 years and 60
percent for remarried couples (Borden). These figures exceeded 50
percent in 2006. Statistics have been reported to be even greater
outside of the United States (Divorce). According to cases disclosed
by divorce attorneys, most marital breakups were the result of
poor communication, financial problems, a lack of commitment, a
dramatic change in priorities and infidelity. To a lesser degree, failed
expectations, unmet needs, addictions, substance abuse, physical,
sexual or emotional abuse and a lack of conflict resolution skills
account for most others. In addition, dissimilarities, pressure to

marry, short acquaintanceship, premarital sex and dysfunctional family backgrounds on the part of one or both partners are attributed (Divorce Form).

Divorce is the household word of our times. People have become disposable. I am appalled when I happen upon books and talks that promote separation. I once expressed my concerns to my friend's former fiancée, saying how I had hoped that their marriage would be a successful one. "We can always get a divorce," was her answer. It is shame that we should be expendable to our mates and spouses.

I hate divorce, says the Lord God of Israel (MI. 2:13-2:16). Marriage is a binding relationship entered into in the presence of God. It is a commitment, an oath before God, family, friends and each other to love and care for each other in sickness and in health and sadness as well as joy, as long as they both shall live, till death do them part. These words were not meant to be taken lightly. Your bride or groom broke a promise, a covenant.

It's Ten O' Clock. Do You Know Where Your Spouse Is?

TWO-FACED ☺ ☹

"And I thought that creep loved me!" May Day shouted in disgust in Ian Fleming's *A View to a Kill*. "You're not the only one he double crossed," responded a sympathetic James Bond. "It doesn't make any sense," you cry out in disbelief. "How could he do that to me?" you ponder. "Why would he buy me such thoughtful gifts if he didn't care?" you desperately try in vain to reason. It is no wonder that you were in complete and utter shock when they practically pushed you out the door.

Mine own familiar friend, in whom I trusted, hath lifted up his heel against me (Ps. 41:9). Lyle's engagement ring to Jane may have amounted to six thousand dollars, but it did not amount to anything else. Alex's ring to his receiver was just a ploy to dupe him into believing that he was in it for the long run. It was not long after that he telephoned him only to find out that he had been given the wrong number and false information. Perhaps those presents were wrapped with ulterior motives. *The gifts of a bad man bring no good with them,* philosopher Euripides once said. Even the wise and responsible mother of the Robinson family in Irwin Allen's *Lost in Space* naively assumed innocence on the part of an alien visitor who had bestowed a bouquet of flowers, ignorant of the man's true intentions of kidnapping her children. "I'll bet you say that to all the guys/girls!"

That romantic trip for two might have been something that he could just have easily taken without you. Perhaps it was something that could have already been on his agenda, and you were just along for the ride and company. "But she said that she loved me!" Talk is cheap, and actions lie louder than words, as we all too often witness in the phony politics of any employment or governing institution. An understanding and acknowledgement of this stark reality is vital in minimizing the resultant shock and disbelief that accompany abandonment. It is easy for us to believe what we want to believe, for actions and attitudes of love and affection feed our ego and appetite for security.

It took an unusually short amount of time for Rich to replace his wife of thirty years and for Eric to find another wife with two children after abandoning his own. It is not uncommon to hear stories about husbands and wives leading double lives. One spouse eventually learns that the other has been concurrently illegally married to somebody else even years later. She said that she was working in the office late on Mondays, Wednesdays, Fridays and alternate weekends. She told you that you were the only man in her life but that she was only available every other weekend. He did not want you to call on certain days during particular hours, and through no fault of your own you heeded his wishes only to be rudely awakened by the latent truth. One who imposes time and telephone call limitations should be suspect from the start.

Carol had Dick convinced that her former husband was Bluebeard himself. She made great first impressions, succeeding in winning people over to her side and believing her sob stories. Penelope was a talented performer who could cry phony tears of sorrow and disappointment on cue. Lee could look Tristan straight in the face and tell him what he wanted to hear one moment, and then stab him right in the back the next. Dave was very crafty as well, knowing how to make each of his three girlfriends believe that she was special and the only one in his life. Deception is any attempt or disposition to lead into error or cause someone to believe what is false, to mislead (Zimmerman). In another *Lost in Space* episode, the Robinson family is duped into assisting a tall handsome, friendly and generous gold-colored stranger in his war against his ugly and unfriendly enemy, the Xenon. Little did they know that this imposter was actually an evil and hideous creature underneath who was also planning to destroy the Robinsons all along. "All too often, people are taken in by good looks, gifts and surface gestures," preaches the injured Xenon at the conclusion of the episode. You do not know what was really lurking behind those pretentious smiles and sweet nothings that they whispered in your ear. Perhaps she actually breathed a sigh of relief when you left her apartment after a date to which you were so privileged. There might have been another character behind the scenes. He might not have been loving you all of that time but simply tolerating you. If she talked about her own friends, family and coworkers behind their backs, then you do not know what he was saying about you in your absence. Did your child's teacher ever invite you in for a sneak preview of your child only to have to call the school psychologist and the nurse who had to resuscitate you with smelling salts?

Charm can be false. *There are many deceivers born into the world* (2 Jo.7). People do not always mean what they say or say what they mean. They can be quite deceptive, posing a phony facade of smiles making it all appear wonderful. If you are not of like mind, then it

Yet *still* we hug the dear deceit

Milton

may be difficult for you to fathom. You might have been shocked by someone else's other side. You could probably list the names of three to five people whom you have known who seemingly betrayed or deceived you with their superficial charm, talk, looks and personalities. He might have only appeared to love you. Users and deceivers lie, change their stories and frequently contradict themselves. Their actions do not necessarily coincide with the words that they speak. They will put on a dramatic and convincing performance, telling you that they cannot stop thinking about you, yet telephone you only once a week, and they will almost always keep you on ice with common and convenient phrases such as "As soon as" and "One day." Perhaps you really did not know the person behind the facade, his true colors. The answers reveal the truth about the love of your life. Indeed, they might have been the love of your life, but were you the love of theirs?

User Friendly

You have dinner reservations for 7 p.m. You are hoping to meet her at her apartment at 6 p.m. and chat over a drink. Her only telephone call to you all week is a call at 5 p.m. to tell you that she will not be ready till 7 p.m. You telephone the restaurant, and graciously they allot you more time. You bide the extra hour making out some bills, straightening up the apartment, and then you leave. You meet her at her apartment at 7 p.m. She is still not ready. By 7:30 p.m., she is all dressed up and ready to go. You spend $150 taking her to a nice restaurant. She never takes the time to prepare a home- cooked meal.

You are a complete gentleman. You open the car door for her, but she does not have the courtesy to open the lock on your side. You are driving in your car as usual.

You arrive at the restaurant, apologizing profusely to the Matre De for being so late. He quickly seats you. The menus arrive. She orders the most expensive entrée, an appetizer, dessert, a before-dinner drink, wine and an after-dinner drink.

You do most of the talking during dinner. You tell her about your day and ask her about hers, but she divulges very little.

The check arrives. She offers to put something toward the bill. You thank her and turn down her offer. She promptly agrees and puts her wallet away. Tomorrow morning she will insist on paying the $10 bill for breakfast at the local coffee shop.

It is now Sunday morning, and she keeps her promise to treat you to breakfast. You feel uncomfortable and order the least expensive breakfast special–and so does she.

You go out for the day, but you feel pressured because she wants you to be on your way home by 5 p.m., so she can do her chores and prepare for work the next day. You go to a museum and then walk through the gift shop. You see something that you know she will love, and you surprise her with it even though it is a bit pricy. She also has a surprise for you–a very inexpensive refrigerator magnet. She hints coyly at another item, which you buy for her at the drop of a hat.

Lunch has you seated at another very nice restaurant with another nice-sized bill. "I'd offer to pay half," she chuckles, "but I know that you would say, 'No.'"

You return to her apartment at 4:30 p.m., embrace and watch a little TV–while she watches the clock. At 5 p.m. she reminds you that she has things to do and has to wake up early. As you are putting on your coat and gloves, you are anticipating a request that you call as soon as you have arrived home safely. She fails to make this request. She also fails to thank you for the dinner, the lunch, the gifts, the outing and for a wonderful weekend.

She did not open the car door lock on your side on the way back to her apartment.

The next day, you call her at work to ask if she had a nice time. She picks up the phone and answers quite loudly, "Hi, sweetie!" loud enough so that everyone in the office knows that a man is on the line. You will arrange to meet her at her job for lunch one afternoon, and she will go out of her way to make sure that she is seen with you by all of her coworkers and supervisors. "What happened to John?" they will ask her. "Who?" she will insensitively reply. Meanwhile, despite your hopes and dreams, you were merely her latest fling only to be succeeded by another.

He betrayed me;
   he broke his promises.
His words are as soothe as lotion,
   but underneath are daggers.
Psalm 55:20-21

Signs of a User

(From the experiences and testimonies of over one hundred correspondents)

- *Exploits your generosity*

- *Wants you around at his convenience & his benefit*

- *Frequently changes mind*

- *Smooth talker*

- *Parasitic*

- *Keeps you believing*

- *Pompous*

- *Makes frequent apologies*

- *Makes promises and doesn't keep them*

- *Unavailable*

Additional Signs of a User

- *Always says the right thing at the right time*

- *Exploits your sincerity & good nature*

- *Manipulates with guilt*

- *Presumptuous*

- *Takes more than she gives*

- *Makes frequent excuses*

- *Exploits your trust*

- *Braggart*

- *False reputation of glibness & charm*

- *Leads you on*

- *Two-faced*

- *Untrustworthy*

- *Makes a good first impression*

- *Egotistical*

- *Selfish*

- *Unappreciative*

Marry above thy match and thou shall get a master, warned Benjamin Franklin. "Marry her if you will, my son, but never fall in love with her, urged Nina Foch to Charlton Heston in Cecil B. De Mille's *The Ten Commandments*. Grandpa used to say that your spouse should not be as wise as you. He also forewarned against becoming involved with older partners. Most importantly, he stressed, the person whom you marry should love you more than you love them. Until I made the mistake of meeting a person who was one up on me on all three, especially the age, I could not understand his reasoning. I thought that he was being old-fashioned and prejudiced. An older man or woman who has ten to fifteen years up on you will have that many years of shrewdness over you as well, and if you are a young, naive, inexperienced and gullible, then you are vulnerable to manipulation and deceit.

Users seize on innocence. They exploit, manipulate and play on it. They are very wise and know how to make very good first impressions. Users are sharp and extremely convincing. They hide their true intentions with charm. However, fair weather friends such as these run for cover at the first sign of precipitation, and trial and tribulation ultimately reveal their deceit, whether it is a called bluff or a crisis that arises just when you need them the most. Users have the gift of gab, and about the only other people whom they cannot deceive are others such as themselves. Eventually their act does become more and more obvious to others, and the reputation that they had quickly established soon begins to tarnish. Nobody is without flaw and none can please everybody; thus, if the man or woman whom you introduce to the world is received with universal approval, then you need to question this person's sincerity.

Bill contributes very little of his salary to his hard-working wife who struggles to maintain the mortgage on their house. Most of his money goes to his parents and relatives in Europe. Sandy is putting Pat through college. Said Sir Walter Raleigh, *Be not made an ass to carry the burdens of others*. Users are generally parasitic to society at large, seeking and devising schemes that will earn them the most for putting out the least. They may seek multiple, simultaneous partners, holding onto those who bring them the most return and letting go of those who do not. In the meantime, they will feed off of whatever you can offer until something "better" comes along. Friends liken this charade to their "shopping around" while you are selfishly kept within arm's reach. Meanwhile, they keep you within their grasp, playing you with promises and guilt trips, until they have finally had their fill of you, justifying their actions with lame excuses or keeping silent, leaving you second-guessing yourself.

What striking a contrast to perhaps a person who is giving–giving to you, to charity and to himself. You want someone who gives more than he takes, who pays his debts and who works for a living, rather than one who takes from you, from others and whose primary sources of income are exaggerated accidents and phony lawsuits. A better choice would be someone who is unselfish and unspoiled, a man who works his hands raw, a woman with good business savvy and an individual who hustles two and three jobs. If these preceding descriptions did not match you former partner(s), or if you find that you always put out more than you get back, then you may be allowing users into your life who are going to take advantage of you and exploit your generosity until a product with more monetary value comes his or her way. Users are colorful and crafty. They know how to say the right thing at the right time. They say exactly what you want to hear. They are also equally effective in shifting blame. Users pose as sincere, free spirits without a care in the world. They paint the picture-perfect wedding, but the moment you call them on it they brush you off.

What knowing judgment, or what piercing Eye,
Can Man's mysterious Maze of Falsehood try?
Man only knows the Cunning of his Kind:
Then heed ye Fair, e'er you their Cunning prove,
And think of Treach'ry, while they talk of Love.
Poor Richard's Almanack

Diversity

Whoever decided that sensitivity was a weakness was obviously not sensitive. Opposites may attract but not for long (Pearsall 189). Consider your occupations. Each field draws a certain type of individual. A social worker and an educator will probably share the same sensitive, open-minded dispositions; however, their values might conflict with the more rigid and introverted style of an accountant or computer programmer. A "tough" pragmatist might consider sensitivity a sign of weakness rather than a gift. If you met a man or woman with a traditional view of masculinity vs. femininity, then she might have thought that you were not "man enough." He might have been threatened by your assertiveness. "Real men don't eat quiche." "A woman flying an airplane, you must be kidding!" You may have been teased for your little library of inspirational literature by the "strong" "realist" who still believes that religion is an "opiate of the masses." Did he angrily and callously tell you to "snap out of it" when you broke down in front of him with uncontrollable tears?

The person whom you choose to marry should also be your friend. *Friendship often ends in love*, said Charles Caleb Colton, *but never does love end in friendship*. You should esteem and respect the other as well as appreciate and cherish each other (Knox). There should be emotional affection toward each other in addition to physical attraction, but there needs to be more to the relationship than physical attraction and sex. You need to be supportive of each other, understand each other and share similar values (Webster's New World Dictionary and Thesaurus: 2: 378). *To cement a new friendship, especially between persons of a different social world,* said Cornelia Otis Skinner, *a spark with which both were secretly charged must fly from person to person, and cut across the accidents of place and time.*

Personal differences may be novel initially; however, they ultimately clash.

Annie: *"You've been out of your room."*
Paul: *"No, I haven't!"*
Annie: *"Paul, my little ceramic penguin in the study always faces due south."*

Kathy Bates and James Caan in *Misery*

Can't See the Forest from the Trees

She is preoccupied with cleanliness, obsessed with germs and has phobias about using public lavatories.

He is a chronic control seeker, scheduling everything in his life, from housecleaning to sex. Laundry time is 12 noon sharp. He has an inordinate need for organization, perhaps stocking the foods in the pantry according to alphabetical or size order.

He is very private, withholding his telephone number from acquaintances and even family.

They are walking contradictions, making promises one moment and changing their minds the next. One day they love you, and the next day they do not. He invites you to move in with him–then throws you out a month later. She tells you that she loves you–and never wants to see you again. She has moved more than five times in the last six years and is yet to hold down a steady job.

He has been overly suspicious and jealous from the start. You interpreted it as love when it was nothing more than control, possessiveness and mistrust, for he would have promptly seized on another opportunity in his favor had it arisen.

She can be charming when she wants to be. She lives in an out of the way, secluded, desolate area in the middle of nowhere, where the only neighbor is not even within line-of-sight distance.

She had not invited a visitor into her home in years until now, playing nursemaid to an injured writer whom she "rescued" from an automobile accident. She had been kind and sweet to him up until she found out that her favorite author killed off her adored character in the final sequel to a literary series. Now she is a whole other person altogether. All of this time, she had been lying to him about telephoning his literary agent and the local hospital about his health and whereabouts; meanwhile, her phone is nothing more than a hollow shell. He is now terrified, bedridden and painfully aware that he is trapped in the house with a lunatic. Actress Kathy Bates portrays Annie Wilkes, a crazed fan of successful author Paul Sheldon. Possessing a dual personality, Wilkes suddenly switches from a kind, gentle woman to a homicidal maniac in the 1990 film *Misery,* similar to the 1960 horror *Psycho*, played by the late Tony Perkins. Even toward the end of this thriller, Wilkes tells Sheldon that she loves him–and wants to kill him with a .32.

They leave a wake of destruction and misery wherever they roam and whomever they encounter, acknowledge behaviorists (Tiscali). He has been virtually setting the stage for an inevitable curtain closing, playing along and cleverly fooling you into believing that he actually loved and cared, while concealing his true colors, motives and intentions. He was a figurative Jack the Ripper, and it was simply a matter of time before he would put a knife to your heart, too. If you could only be there to warn the next victim before she too suffers the same fate as you did.

Friends raised eyebrows when you told them about him and could not understand why you entered into a commitment with him in the first place. *He who trusts in his own mind is a fool* (Pr. 28:26). You did not see what they saw. You loved this person, made excuses for him, defended him and sympathized. You alienated yourself from your friends and family, and then you alienated yourself from yourself. Over time, you forsook your own identity and became his carbon copy.

Liken a dysfunctional or abusive relationship to a young child being brought up in an all-encompassing irregular household by a maladjusted guardian in the absence of his parents. He grows up in an unconventional environment where antisocial behavior is the norm and knows no other. Any subsequent unorthodox people with eccentric or irregular habits and behaviors with whom the child becomes acquainted will henceforth be familiar, akin to a poisonous false sense of security. He will know no other. He will fail to notice peculiarities such as obsessive compulsive behavior, overcautiousness, frequent and extreme mood shifts, excessive demands, uncalled for and unproductive criticism, harsh judgments and physical and psychological mistreatment.

A traumatic experience with parental authority, asserts Stanislav Grof, M.D., *can contaminate all future relationships with superiors and other people in positions of authority.* *Women, Sex and Addiction's* Charlotte D. Kasl, Ph. D. maintained that *we pick people like our parents and try to change them.* Says Kasl, for *most people who come from dysfunctional families the underlying goal of the psyche in choosing partners is often to address unfinished business from childhood.* *If you accept that you cannot change a cold person and give up trying, two things will happen.* *You will feel grief for the loss of the father who was cold and you will be free to choose a more loving partner* (Primal Page).

It is such a paradox that rational people allow themselves to be made the scapegoat for the outlandish actions of the irrational, believing that they themselves are ill, while those who are clinically unsound are unable to admit it or realize their own illness. Falling victim to abandonment by the mentally troubled carries an extra sting, for in falling in love blindly with a man or woman with an antisocial personality disorder, we naturally project our own expectations and societal standards of normalcy and rationality to one who does not follow the norm. *Alienated sociopaths,* for example, do not have the ability to love, empathize or affiliate with another person (World Book, Inc.). They have a cold, callous attitude toward human suffering, possess personality traits akin to *psychopaths* and can cleverly conceal their hostility behind a false façade of glibness and superficial charm (All Watchers). This can prove to be emotionally traumatic for the naive and unsuspecting partner who at the drop of a hat can be disposed of suddenly and easily and left bewildered, trying to pick up the pieces for months or even years later. Believing that they were cheated by society, they are chronic complainers and have no problems making their victims the scapegoat (Primal Page). They are indifferent to dating and marriage relationships and tend to live life in a shell. Sociopaths and their psychopathic brothers are walking lies (Webster's New World Dictionary and Thesaurus 2: 145+).

Among the characteristics that constitute mental disability is impractical, illogical, unreasonable, foolish, erratic or unusual behavior with such unsoundness of mind or lack of understanding, preventing one from having the mental capacity required to enter into a relationship. These are persons generally known to have antisocial, personality or mood disorders, for example, *sociopaths, psychotics* and *schizophrenics* (Merriam-Webster Collegiate Dictionary 11: 293+).

The more severe forms of personality disorders, *sociopath* or *psychopathic,* are characterized by a surface and superficial charm and a lack of remorse, shame or guilt. Being incapable of genuine bonding and human attachment, they feign emotions of warmth, joy, love and compassion, all of which serve as an ulterior motive (Merriam-Webster Collegiate Dictionary 11: 293+).

People with personality disorders may be narcissistic, not perceiving that anything is wrong with them, and portray themselves to the world as the model of perfection, confidence, bliss and conventionality. *Their ways are unstable and they knoweth it not* (Pr. 5:6). At their core, however, lies deep-seated anger and hostility that stem from a legacy of early unresolved conflicts, dependencies and aggressions that are repressed and displaced onto other people, namely their lovers, spouses and children. As a result of this, their charming and hospitable public persona is often completely different than the less desirable persona that they save for their husband, wife or child (Metcalf). They occasionally appear upon casual inspection to be successful members of the community at large, presenting a technical appearance of sanity and conventionality quite often with very high intellectual capacities. They tend to think "logically" and are often applauded for their "rationality" and victory over human emotions (Home Data West). Says David Borenstein, *Feelings are not supposed to be logical, and dangerous is the person who has rationalized his* (Primal Page). These dissentients do not perceive others around them as people but merely as targets and opportunities to be used and exploited, having victims and accomplices who end up as victims ultimately. They are egotistical and self-righteous. They fail to recognize the feelings and rights of others and see their self-serving behaviors as permissible. They are unsympathetic toward the suffering. They are callous and lack empathy, unreliable and irresponsible, not concerned about wrecking others' lives and dreams, oblivious or indifferent to the devastation that they cause and unable to empathize with the pain of their victims, having only contempt for others' feelings of distress and readily take advantage of them (Angel). The end always justifies the means. As a result, their victims rationalize their behavior as necessary for their own good, unable to fathom that they would bring them pain or harm. They do not accept blame but blame others, reinforcing passivity, obedience, guilt, shame and feelings of insignificance and worthlessness. They are devoid of conscience, virtue and morality (Tiscali).

According to psychologist Nancy Andreasen, persons who are afflicted with antisocial personality disorders have very noticeable mood changes and may be overly suspicious, cautious and secretive. They may have obsessive-compulsive personalities, attaching great importance to being organized and immaculate. Common obsessions include thoughts of committing violent acts or becoming infected with germs and disease. They strive for perfection and efficiency continually and may spend an inordinate amount of time making lists and schedules. They often make unreasonable and irrational demands on other people, imposing bizarre rules and punishments, and have difficulty expressing their emotions. They are critical of others but have difficulty accepting criticism and are often outraged by insignificant matters yet remaining indifferent and unmoved by injury, death, catastrophe and almost anything else that would upset the mainstream. They are pathological liars, having no problem lying coolly and easily, and it is impossible for them to be truthful on a consistent basis.

Sociopaths are extremely convincing, and language can be used without effort by them to confuse and convince their audience. Rage, physical and verbal abuse, alternating with small expressions of love and approval, produce an addictive cycle for abuser and abused as well as creating despondency and hopelessness in the victim. Control and dominance over a willing victim are their ultimate objectives. They are sexually promiscuous. They have multiple and short-lived, unstable personal relationships and marriages. Having a lack of realistic life plans, they move around frequently, make all-encompassing promises for the future and may have parasitic life styles. Since they are not genuine, neither are their promises. Personality disorders run in families (World Book).

BEWARE OF SERIAL HEARTBREAKERS

Although *the transmission of destructiveness is not intentional*, according to psycho historian Lloyd de Mause, there are people who compulsively seek to hurt others. Their rage is that born of unfulfilled needs as infants. *Incomprehensible pain is forever locked in their souls because of the abandonment they felt as infants*, asserted *High Risk's* Dr. Ken Magid and Carole A. McKelvey. We have all heard horror stories about men and women enticing one another only to commit some unspeakable act or willfully spreading a harmful or deadly virus. Maybe she held a subconscious vendetta against men. He might have some unfinished business with women. *The hurtful adult was once a hurt child*, de Mause maintained (Primal Page).

You might be drawn to the unconventional, thriving on unpredictability. You may not have wanted to realize the truth. You may have grown accustomed to their eccentric behavior, assimilated it and ceased to recognize it as deviant. Their flippant and bizarre thinking and behavior can engross their unaware victims into an abysmal world of distortion and confusion.

Abuse

"This is my wife," he bantered in front of his friends, "she's not pregnant, just needs to lose a few pounds!" "How will I make it out there alone with three children?"

Mary and Annie were unable to resist their boyfriends' charming and appealing personalities. Their family and friends were also very fond of them and taken in by their happy-go-lucky attitudes and good natures, that was until their weddings. Within a few months following their vows, both women were physically abused and forced to keep away from their family and friends, especially male friends. Both underwent very traumatic divorces and are emotionally scarred. "I ran away from him, taking my daughter with me," Annie revealed. "Nobody ever would have expected this from him." *There are no ugly loves nor handsome prisons*, said Benjamin Franklin, and emotional or physical abuse simply has no place in a relationship.

Physical abuse occurs in a predictable cycle. It starts with the *build-up phase*, where the tension builds, followed by the *stand-over phase*, wherein there is an increase of verbal attack. Next is the *explosion phase*, in which a violent outburst occurs, followed by the *remorse phase,* whereby the offender blames the victim. In the *pursuit phase*, the batterer promises never to do it again. Finally, there is the *honeymoon phase*, similar to the eye of a hurricane, whereof the abusive person assures the victim that all is well (Hometown Companion).

There was once a baby show among the Animals in the forest. All the proud mammals from far and near brought their babies. Mother Monkey proudly presented her baby among the other contestants. There was a laugh when the Animals saw the ugly flat-nosed, hairless, pop-eyed little creature. "Laugh if you will," said the Mother Monkey, "I know that he is the prettiest, the sweetest, and the dearest darling in the world."

Aesop

Although rage and violence coupled with small expressions of love are signs of physical abuse, emotional or psychological abuse, though notably subtle, does share many common characteristics. It can take the form of subtle or blatant emotional and verbal attacks. Whether it is physical or psychological, the ultimate motive behind the abusive partner is control. They may apologize and promise never to repeat their actions; however, these apologies and assurances are insincere. Abusers are manipulative and can deliberately create situations that leave the victim feeling powerless and dependent. They are covert about their conduct, their public persona almost always being contrary to that which their spouses or lovers witness. They have deep-seated mental disorders and are often unremorseful for the deep and long-lasting emotional wounds that they inflict, perceiving themselves as victims to excuse their behavior and actions. Batterers seek dominance and control. They scratch, hit, throw things, knock down tables, rip things and smash windows, becoming whole different persons. Psychological abuse may take somewhat subtler forms, for example, disrespectful and disparaging remarks made toward family and friends (Home Data West).

Physical domestic violence accounts for 21 percent of violent crimes experienced by women and 2 percent of the violence experienced by men. In 1992 alone, 1,414 women were homicidal victims to assault and battery as well as 637 men (Home Data West).

You can guess what happened to people long ago if you listen to what they say they felt the past week, said Doyle P. Henderson (Primal Page). We are products of our environment (Willford). We are victims of victims. The hurt, hurt and the loved, love. Therefore, never criticize another until, as the Native Americans say, you have walked a mile in his moccasins. It may be something beyond their control. This was not necessarily about you. You really do not know the whole story. Many offenders have a history of drug or alcohol abuse, and the most abusive offenders tend to have severe emotional problems (Woman Abuse Prevention). Numerous offenders were abused and had unfulfilled needs as children, being rejected by the mother; thus, an attitude of compassion and sympathy might be in order instead of one of anger or vengeance (4Woman). *What could be more pathetic than a child crying for want of mothering and the mother striking out at it because she is not mothering her in answering to her longing,* posed psychologist Jean Liedoff (Primal Page)?

Most people still believe that it is their fault when they are abused, convinced that "If only..." or "If I hadn't..." then they would not have brought it on. Abusive people foster co dependence in their victims (Woman Abuse Prevention). This process is gradual, subtle and insidious. One who is infatuated with someone risks the possibility of an emotional let-down of paramount proportions if s/he is disappointed in the end. Dr. Paul Pearsall's *opponent process theory* states that without exception, *if enough time passes, elation will always be followed by the affective afterimage of letdown* (142). Among other things, her identity, personality, confidence and happiness slowly slip away, gradually making her lose trust in herself, her opinions, judgments, assertions and decisions (Metcalf). He may be left feeling angry, depressed and suicidal (Sylvia). Depression, addiction and the compulsion toward self-harm are some of the psychological distress that recipients of abusive partners endure (Gaudette; Larsen).

The following is a list of common abuse signs (South Coast Today; Gaudette; Larsen; World Book, Inc.; T. Buddy; Time for Hope; Woman Abuse Prevention):

Signs of Abuse

- *Wakes you up at all hours of the night*

- *Isolates you from family and friends*

- *Embarrasses you in front of others*

- *Blames you for everything*

- *Rubs salt in old wounds*

- *Unavailable*

- *Fosters insecurity & uncertainty*

- *Lies to you*

- *Unappreciative*

- *Impossible to please*

- *Does not listen to you*

- *Hits*

More Abuse Signs

- *Self-centered*
- *Humiliates you*
- *Keeps track of your activities*
- *Questions your sexuality*
- *Gets annoyed over trivial matters*
- *Judgmental*
- *Pushes*
- *Sadistic*
- *Impedes your success and happiness*
- *Controlling*
- *Emasculating*
- *Disrespectful*
- *Withholds sex as punishment*
- *Cruel*
- *Insensitive*
- *Neglectful*
- *Belittles your sexual performance*
- *Accusatory*
- *Critical*
- *Scares or threatens*
- *Damages your prized possessions*
- *Has a history of failed relationships*
- *Jealous*
- *Hurtful-physically or emotionally*
- *Spits*
- *Pinches*
- *Fosters dependency*

The list goes on; however, the signs listed on the previous pages are the most common reported by victims of abusive spouses and partners. These and other very well-written articles on the subject are available through the Internet.

Honeymooners and Faultfinders

Why is an attractive girl like that still single after all of these years?" They are late in their ages, feeling sorry for themselves and endlessly pouting that they "just never met the right one," individuals whom friends, family and coworkers try to match up fruitlessly. "There just isn't anyone decent out there!" they gripe. "I'll never find anyone!"

Your former partner might have been a man who mistakes initial romance and infatuation for genuine love. She may have been a woman who seeks additional honeymoon experiences, fixes and rushes with successive others when the infatuation is over with one partner, claiming that the relationship just "fizzled." Love and commitment, however, begin after the honeymoon. Relationships and marriages are not easy, and couples who have remained together for many years certainly continue to have their share of difficulty and struggle, but if two people love each other, then they will make the effort willingly to work it out together. She might have been a hopeless romantic who flows in and out of relationships incessantly, looking for "The Perfect One." They find fault with everybody (except themselves), discarding one partner after another, and you were simply a matter of time. We believe everything that they recount about their former "villains" and tend to judge them harshly. There are two sides to every tale, however, and one should never judge their date's previous men and women solely on the basis of their own testimony. It would prove to be quite revealing if we could get their side of the story. It is too bad that we cannot get references.

Various factors may account for the fickleness of a honeymooner or faultfinder, but whatever the cause, it is a mirror of one's own unstable and insatiable nature, stemming from a childhood of neglect and injury. It is actually the chase that many of them love and not the person himself (World Book). "Alexander wept when there were no more worlds to conquer." Success and accomplishment are often accompanied by boredom and discontent unless a subsequent goal is sought after. James thrived on challenge and insecurity. It was no coincidence that he never stayed with somebody nice or available, someone with whom he probably would have sustained a permanent relationship. Even his career in theater was exemplary of his need for instability and uncertainty. Pliny the Younger wrote some two thousand years ago that an object in possession seldom retains the same charm that it had in pursuit. Wanting is better than having. For many of these single people, it is a fear of intimacy or attachment. Still, others are yet to admit to themselves that they really prefer bachelorhood to marriage. They are perpetual seekers who suddenly develop a severe case of cold feet right when things start getting too close and then quickly boot you out of their lives altogether with their frostbitten heels. For others, the kill is an ego booster, and some people flounder from one relationship to another, endlessly searching for the proverbial pot of gold that lies somewhere at the end of the rainbow. For the man or woman whose hunter suffered from the *Casanova syndrome*, his or her value was only in the conquest. It is just unfortunate that you had to play the role of stepping stone for their selfish needs and pursuits, and unfortunately, others yet to come will also pay the price of their flippancy (Primal Page).

PROCEED WITH CAUTION

Single White Female, 46, playful and friendly seeks SWM.

Be cautious of whom you are meeting and where you are meeting them. It is generally safer if you have known them for some time rather than taking your chances with strangers through the personals and barflies at the clubs and taverns. Most successful relationships and marriages begin as friendships between people who know each other well.

Be especially leery of meeting strangers through the Internet. With more people claiming to be that whom they are not, predators disguising themselves as teenagers to catch the unsuspecting adolescent and others expressing obscenities and performing a myriad of perverted acts, meeting people through random means has become a risky endeavor. You might be better off meeting people through family, friends and coworkers or by joining a more exclusive, higher cost dating service rather than leave your emotional or physical well-being to chance.

Shortly after they met in a bar, Lenny discovered Lila's maddening idiosyncrasies in *The Heartbreak Kid.* He thought that he loved her and knew her after a brief courtship only to learn that he had made a mistake by smashing that champagne flute too soon. He grew annoyed by her need for constant affection and reassurance, grew impatient with the exorbitant amount of time that it took her to get ready to go out and was turned off by her slovenly manners. Courtney should have known Ariel a little better before deciding to move in with him just two weeks after meeting him in a Manhattan nightclub. Russ thought that he knew Gene until drugs and promiscuity entered the apartment. Buzz rushed into a marriage after a brief and intoxicating relationship with Joy, whom he met at the cocktail lounge where she worked. It should not have come as a shock for him to learn that she was an alcoholic after coming down from his high. This is not to say that you will not find the spirit of your heart's content in a pub, but a good wine comes with age.

Affairs-And Other 'Safe' Arrangements

"Collect call to Australia, please."

"Who's this, your mother?" "My husband doesn't get home until nine." Across-the-mile romances, older and younger mates, affairs with the married or engaged, perhaps they were short-term arrangements doomed from the start, never intended to go anywhere in the first place.

"Why does the blind man's wife paint herself?" queried Benjamin Franklin. If your spouse had been having an affair with your best friend, then rest assured that you are not alone. Most "safe," short-term arrangements such as affairs with friends, married or engaged people, flings with older or younger people not intended to get beyond a short-term series of physical encounters, long-distance romances and flings with divorcees, stem from a fear of intimacy or commitment. These relationships remain safe until one partner discovers that he or she wants something more from the other. At this point, the other partner who simply could not live without you when you were unavailable is suddenly frightened and dashes very quickly in the opposite direction. If the person who decided to leave you already had a history of short-term encounters with people or individuals whom they thought were unavailable, then it was just a matter of time before your time with them would also draw to a conclusion. Perhaps they might have sensed that you were safe for them initially, but then time brought you closer and interested in something more permanent.

In Praise of Older Men and Women– And Younger Ones

Pete was dating a woman who was old enough to be his mother. Virginia dated somebody old enough to be her grandfather. Men and women are attracted to older partners for their experience, wisdom, confidence, and especially for a younger man, sexual expertise. These assumptions and expectations do not always come to fruition, for not all aged people are necessarily experienced, wise, confident and sexually sophisticated. Unforeseen problems could also arise later on down the road. A ten- or even fifteen-year age gap may not be much of an issue with which to deal at forty or fifty, but health problems, compatibility and sexual performance may put a strain on the relationship in later years. An older partner, on the other hand, should be cautious about dating younger people who date them out of convenience and without any intention of commitment.

Instead of focusing on the loss of your partner here and now, try looking at what might have awaited you in the future. Visualize your forty- or fifty-year-old former mother or father figure ten to fifteen years from now. Abigail Van Buren once contended that wine improves with age but only if the grapes were good in the first place. As Suzanne Somers said, "We sag, sweat and complain when we are going through menopause."

Understanding It: Home Is Where the Heart Is

Whether you were one of the few to be spared the rod of emotional, verbal and physical abuse, or even if you were a mere spectator, childhood abuse can have long-term serious emotional and psychological side effects. According to Dr. Sigmund Freud's *theory of repetition compulsion, or transference, it is the compulsion of the human psyche to repeat traumatic events and to resolve childhood conflicts, dependencies and aggressions from abusive home, school and social figures by displacing them onto a substitute object, most notably our partners* (Felluga). Simply stated, it is the mind's self-martyring mission in life to seek abusive people and situations, to pay back old debts, cutting off the nose to spite the face–a masochistic need. Therefore, whether we realize it or not (and we usually do not), we tend to attract and be attracted to the same types of people. An analyst can work with you to determine your relationship choices and the motives behind them. We seek the familiar even if it is poisonous. Significant others in your life might have exemplified or epitomized your parents, siblings or childhood pedagogues. Even some of your friends and acquaintances may share some of the undesirable traits and behaviors of your former mates. If your own self-image is lacking, then you are also more likely to fall prey to unhealthy people and unhealthy entanglements.

Recall your early grade school experiences. Your elementary, intermediate or high school environment may have influenced the decisions that you made and the people whom you allowed into your life. Perhaps you have discovered that many of your choices in mates were similar to your educators or other authority figures. If an only child's mother left home at an early age, for example, leaving her in the care of a sexually abusive or alcoholic father, then she may develop a very big fear of abandonment, thus remaining aloof in relationships, which will most often be short lived. She will unlikely be able to form any real bonds. Others' partners may not necessarily be unkind; however, they may be unavailable most of the time, much the same as their parents might have been. Relationships stemming from this experience might include long-distance romances and younger partners who could never fully commit. A man or woman's adult figures and childhood relationships are good indicators of the length and quality of the relationship that you might expect. However, we are blinded by familiarity, as an old Aesop fable reminds us.

The Stockholm Syndrome

On August 23, 1973, four Swedes held in a bank vault for six days during a robbery became attached to their captors. Initially fearing harm from their captors, the hostages sought to win their favor in an almost childlike way through support and cooperation. In sparing their lives, the perpetrators were perceived to be benevolent by the group. Time bred familiarity, and the captives became kindred with the gunmen, no longer perceiving their motives and actions as diabolical. Through denial, the four repressed the malevolent reality in which they were encompassed and directed their abomination toward the rescuers, ironically (The Peace Encyclopedia).

The Stockholm syndrome is an emotional attachment, a bond of interdependence between captive and captor that develops when the latter threatens the former's life, deliberates but does not kill him. The relief resulting from the removal of the overwhelming threat of death and disaster generates intense feelings of gratitude and fear that combine to make the captive reluctant to display negative feelings toward the captor. The captor, in denying his feelings, namely fear and self-pity, along with the brutal reality of his circumstances, will shift all emphasis away from himself and toward the culprit, thereby becoming more and more familiar with and accepting of the victimizer's mentality and his expectations (The Peace Encyclopedia). Likewise, the victim of an abusive lover or spouse, in denying the undesirable and destructive realities of her relationship with her partner (akin to Freud's application of *repetition-compulsion* to come to grips with and master unpleasant experiences through creative rationalization), centers on her beneficent gestures and becomes acclimated to her mentality and her standards, thereby becoming oblivious to them. In fact, similar to a captor or terrorist, an abusive partner may intentionally plant and nurture the seeds of adoration in the heart of his victim with acts of kindness and generosity to maintain this deception of love and sincerity, along with dependency, lack of initiative and the inability to act, think and decide independently, as a method of control. Like captors after a prolonged period of time, abused partners eventually develop a psychological attachment toward their abusive significant others (World Book). We were all warned at home to stay away from kids at school who had a "bad influence" on us.

Freud asserted that *it is actually one's own ego that one loves in love and not the object of our love.* He maintained that the human psyche's need to love need not be directed at only one object of affection but by allowing this love to protrude to all beings equally. Christ likewise preached love for all people. We must recognize the paradox that our need to *be* loved is actually a need *to* love on a subconscious level. Once acknowledged, humankind can serve as a substitute for the lost recipient through transference (Felluga).

It comes down to how you feel about yourself, and it is widely known among members of Narcotics Anonymous and other twelve-step recovery programs that many of the problems which we encounter arise from an inability to accept ourselves on a deep level (Recovery and Relapse). Unable to accept ourselves, we perpetuate a lifelong quest to gain the acceptance of others, expecting them to provide us with the love and acceptance that we are unable to provide for ourselves (Being in a Dependent Relationship). Freudian psychologists claim, however, that this adoration and approval that we so futilely try to secure from others is actually a desire to win the favor of our parents (Felluga). Becoming a successful attorney, getting that Ph. D., driving around in that Mercedes or meeting the ideal person, then, is a vain attempt to impress them and not our peers to whom we wish to become desirable. Women with compulsive pregnancies, for example, may bear children out of a need to live up to the fantasy of becoming the perfect mother, more so than out of sincere desire for a baby.

Your acquired need to gravitate toward the familiar, whether it is to win acceptance, avenge a parent, relive trauma or resolve some other early childhood conflict, is merely perpetuating the pattern of repetition in which you are finding yourself. It is a paradox. If your self-acceptance is at the mercy of hopelessly winning over someone who will never accept you, then you could never hope to accept yourself. If you are compelled to meet people with whom to tie up loose ends, then you will not be free to discover happiness.

Chapter Summary

We tend to attract and be attracted to the same types of people. People who have contempt for us, hurt and deceive us may be part of a pattern of choices in partners that we have subconsciously made for ourselves for years. If we look back, then we will most likely see that our last was not much different from those who came before. Thus, your most recent choice was merely a reflection of a pattern that you have been perpetuating. Harry Stack Sullivan attributed learning disability to *selective attention*, whereby the learner listens only to what is tolerable (Roswell and Natchez 144). Likewise, undesirable memories and realities are successfully blocked out of our minds through denial and repression, leaving an idealized and romanticized impression of our former mates and relationships. We remember what was good and dismiss what was bad. The love and glorification that we have for our partners is a projection of the ideal love and happiness within ourselves, our denial of a reality that we chose not to accept and a reflection of our own need for the comfort of the familiar. Often it is not until the relationship is over that we see our partner's true colors, the side that they did not reveal or that we subconsciously failed to notice. The end was in sight, and the signs were there all along. You failed to see the reality or simply chose not to accept it.

You had the misfortune of getting involved with a person who was clearly an unhealthy choice, but having grown up in an environment where abuse, deceit, manipulation and self-centeredness were the norm, you were blind to a situation that was slowly destroying you and might have done so had it continued.

The mind's compulsion to repeat traumatic events subconsciously compels us to seek people who are abusive or otherwise harmful to our emotional well-being in order to deal with or rectify unresolved adverse conditions and experiences with people from our childhood, most notably parents and educators, though not limited to these exclusively. You thought it acceptable for another person to criticize, abuse, blame, strike, threaten, control and make unreasonable demands; thus, you are perpetuating traumatic feelings, contradictorily, by getting involved with people to whom you have appointed the role of the villain and with whom you are trying to avenge yourself.

The Stockholm syndrome may explain why couples often remain in abusive and harmful relationships, gradually accepting and assimilating the wonton attitudes and behaviors of their antagonists who methodically subvert them through manipulative acts of benevolence and entrapments of dependence; thus, it is not the person with whom we fall in love but what we subconsciously think that the person has provided for or resolved for us (What is Codependence? and Recovery: How will I Know?). *The truth shall set ye free* (Jn. 8:32). Therefore, take responsibility for allowing these people into your life, for extending the relationship, for allowing them to hurt you, and do not repeat risky or undesirable relationship patterns.

Tell me who you love and
I will tell you who you are.
Houssaye

One cold stormy day a Goatherd drove his goats for shelter into a cave, where a number of Wild Goats had also found their way. The Shepherd wanted to make the Wild Goats part of his flock; so he fed them well. But to his own flock, he gave only just enough food to keep them alive. When the weather cleared, and the Shepherd led the Goats out to feed, the Wild Goats scampered off to the hills. "Is that the thanks I get for feeding you and treating you so well?" complained the Shepherd. "Do not expect us to join your flock," replied one of the Wild Goats. "We know how you would treat us later on, if some strangers should come as we did."

Aesop

If you can trust yourself when all men doubt you,
but make allowance for their doubting too...

Rudyard Kipling

CHAPTER II
Do Not Personalize

Nothing others do is because of you.

Don Miguel Ruiz

CHAPTER II: Do Not Personalize

"Mrs. Kramer, in all the years you were married, did your husband ever abuse you in any way?" "No!" "Did he ever abuse his child in any way?" "No!" "Did he ever hit you or beat you?" "No!" "Did he ever fail to provide for you?" "No!" "Did he ever fail to provide for his child?" "No!" "Would you describe your husband as an alcoholic?" "No!" "A heavy drinker?" "No!" "Was he ever unfaithful?" "No!" "Well, I can certainly see why you left him!"

(Court Scene from the Film *Kramer vs. Kramer)*

Our Own Worse Critics
Guilty as Uncharged

It must have been something you did, your parents assumed whenever a new date or prospect did not go well even though they had insufficient evidence to present to the jury to support this accusation or witnesses to take the stand. It is no wonder why we waive the right to a fair trial. "It *must* have been something I did," you conclude, "it's entirely my fault!" "There should be Hell to pay for what *I* did!" "*I* deserve to be severely punished for speaking *my* mind, flogged for having a different opinion and committed for having feelings!" You are guilty of being human. You have appointed yourself your own judge, jury and executioner, pleaded guilty with insufficient evidence for conviction and waived your rights to a fair and impartial trial. We can be so self-deprecating, especially after a breakup, focusing on our imperfections and recalling the undesirable behaviors that we displayed to our partners. They may even capitalize on these deficiencies unscrupulously to justify their actions unjustly, rendering us even more self-annihilating (Messina).

A Lamb stood drinking early one morning on the bank of a woodland stream. That very same morning a hungry Wolf came by farther up the stream, hunting for something to eat. He soon got his eyes on the Lamb. As a rule Mr. Wolf snapped up such delicious morsels without making any bones about it, but this Lamb looked so very helpless and innocent. "How dare you paddle around in my stream and stir up all the mud!" he shouted fiercely. "You deserve to be punished severely for your rashness!" "But, your highness," replied the trembling Lamb, "I cannot possibly muddy the water you are drinking up there. You are upstream and I am down stream." "I have heard that you told lies about me last year!" "How could I have done so?" pleaded the Lamb. "I wasn't born until this year." "Well, then it was someone in your family, but no matter who it was, I do not intend to be talked out of my breakfast."

Aesop

Would've Done the Same Thing to Me

Picture an imaginary encounter with the ex-boyfriend, girlfriend, fiancée or spouse of your former lover. Take this opportunity to commiserate. You would probably have much to ask and much to say. If you told them what happened to you, then in all likelihood their response would be, "Yeah, they did the same thing to me" (Staton). *Go not astray in her path for she hath cast down many wounded* (Pr. 7:25-26). Like a child who quickly disposes of the toy – for which she had hounded her daddy– as soon as a new one grabs her attention, you were not the first, and you shall not be the last.

It is easy to personalize what happened, and the more we esteem another, the greater we internalize. When we love as strongly as we do, we place our significant other up on a pedestal, and if our own self-image is poor, then we can just as easily place ourselves on the bottom of that pedestal and lower. If you have an inflated ego, for example, then you are more likely to personalize your partner's leaving you, assuming that it was something about you, something that *you* did or *you* said. We exaggerate our attitudes and actions, thinking that they are of huge consequence. You are not the center of the universe. They do not perceive you the way you perceive yourself. They did not know you, and you obviously did not know them well enough. Those who matter know you and have accepted you for who you are and what you are not. Those who mind do not know and appreciate you for who and what you are–the good *and* the bad (Messina).

In addition to internalizing, you are also projecting your own narcissistic visualization of yourself, your former partner and the relationship onto his projection screen; meanwhile, the two of you have been watching a different movie. She is not you, and you are not her. You do not know what they were thinking and feeling all of this time. You only know what you think you know, and what you think you know is merely your own image projected onto your own motion picture screen (Felluga). You do not know what their true feelings, motives and intentions were. You only know what yours were. You have probably told a joke before, which you thought was absolutely hilarious, only to find that you were the only one laughing. "I know this great restaurant; you'll love it!" "Now if that movie doesn't get Best Picture..." Think about all of the other times that you drew an unexpected reaction or when you anticipated praise but were criticized and discounted instead of appreciated. Every man and woman marches to the beat of a different tune (FitzMaurice).

We tend to minimize their actions, and like Aesop's fabled gnat who sought pardon from the heedless bull for settling on the tip of one of his horns to take a short rest, we exaggerate our own "misdeeds" as well as our thoughts and attitudes when they are hardly worth a passing glance to others. We readily exonerate them from all of their wrongdoing while unjustly condemning ourselves to a lifelong prison sentence of guilt and self-reproof. Your lover was certainly not a saint either and was most likely too preoccupied with her own quirks, prejudices and self-judgments to be fazed by yours. Their decision may have had nothing to do with you at all. A leopard does not change its spots. This is who they are.

People fall into behavior patterns. What they did to you they have probably done before and will continue to do with each successive encounter. There are many people who manage to stay single all of their lives, perhaps having multiple partners and relationships. If you married a man who had divorced three wives, then it should come as no surprise that you were number four. If she was an older woman who had never been married before, then it was just a matter of time before she left you standing at the altar, too. If your fiancée was an intolerant, obsessive-compulsive, rigid perfectionist, then she could not possibly be compatible with you or anybody else. You could never compete with the myriad of obsessions and compulsions that took precedence in her head. She could not even know you or anybody else—or herself for that matter.

Rejection is not personal (FitzMaurice). They *rejected* you, but they did not reject *you*. It takes a fool to criticize, condemn and complain. A child will reject anybody at all for no reason at all. Any rejection so easily won can hardly be highly valued (Greenburg 98-99), and *tailoring your life to accommodate the opinions and expectations of other people is nothing more than slavery*, suggests Lawana Blackwell. The chances are that it will be quite difficult for one to destroy a deep relationship unless approached in a sufficiently oblique and underhanded manner. Relationships that get off to too hot a start almost always fizzle in the end while those that are given time to simmer will generally stay warm with perseverance.

A Compliment in Disguise

The proof of your personal value and goodness is all around you– your family and friends who know and love you, your colleagues who respect you and your supervisors who count on you. Every knock is a boost, mom's always told you. It is quite possible that he left because *you* were too good for *him*. Your former mate may tend to gravitate toward others such as himself. You might have been rejected by someone in the past only to be shocked at their choice of a successor. She left me for *him*? I had the looks of a peacock, the grace of a swan and the intelligence of an owl, yet he chose an orangutan. Perhaps your little lamb felt that she deserved an orangutan. Maybe your beast knew that he could never live up to the intelligence of an owl. Your lassie might have felt threatened by her Great Dane and needed a puppy dog to leash around. They might have felt that your fox looks would make you prey for the bloodhounds. His manhood might have been threatened by your lioness assertiveness or feline independence. One who is insecure will readily accept someone whom they feel is less adequate, which accounts for the mismatches that we see. A secure person knows his worth. She is also more unlikely to come with excess psychological baggage, increasing the likelihood of a successful, permanent relationship. Cease giving others so much esteem, wisdom and power at the expense of your own.

Strike Three and You're Out⁈
Forgiving Yourself

All-stars make errors on the field. Legendary boxers lose their titles. Gold medalists slip and fall. They put erasers on pencils. Nobody is perfect. You are going to make mistakes. You are going to insult and offend people. You cannot swim in the sea of life without making waves. Even if you were a loving and caring partner, it would not have mattered ultimately. The hare lost the race to the tortoise because the race is not always to the swift.

It is easy to put ourselves on the hot seat. "Maybe if I hadn't…" "If only I had…" We are people and not machines, and if your former mate or spouse could condemn you for your failings, then he or she is not worth your time and investment. Chances are that their criticisms were merely excuses to waltz away from a dance that they had long since choreographed for a closing curtain. Love keeps no record of wrongs. The positives probably outweighed the negatives. Stop punishing yourself. Nobody is perfect. *God* has forgiven you (Mt. 9:2). If "The One" cannot forgive you for your "crimes," then it does not say much about her or him (Willford). Reverse it. They were not perfect. You probably tolerated more from them than most others would have. Perhaps they were not able to hold down a relationship with those who preceded you. They might have been prompt to notice the speck in your eye, highlighting all of your flaws, but were blind to the log in their own (Mt. 7:4). You were certainly willing to forgive them for their shortcomings, yet they were unwilling to respond in kind.

The Good with the Bad

All of us bring a host of undesirable personality traits, behaviors and actions into a relationship as well as gifts, strengths and attributes, and short of physical abuse and perhaps infidelity, imperfection is no grounds for dismissal. If it was, then he or she was just looking for an excuse to leave or searching for something that does not exist. We make mistakes, learn from them, make more mistakes and learn from them (Willford), and we continue to make mistakes infinitely.

There was once an Ass whose Master also owned a Lap Dog. This Dog was a favorite and received many a pat and kind word from his master. Every day the Dog would run to meet the Master, frisking playfully about and leaping up to lick his hands and face. All this the Ass saw with much discontent. The Master hardly ever took any notice of him. Now the Ass got it into his little head that all he had to do to win his Master's favor was to act like the Dog. So one day he left his stable and clattered eagerly into the house. Finding his Master seated at the dinner table, he kicked up his heels and, with a loud bray, pranced giddily around the table, upsetting it as he did so. Then he planted his forefeet on his Master's knees and rolled out his tongue to lick the Master's face, as he had seen the Dog do. But his weight upset the chair, and Ass and man rolled over together in the pile of broken dishes from the table. The Master was much alarmed at the strange behavior of the Ass, and drove him back to the stable. There they left him to mourn the foolishness that had brought him nothing but a sound beating.

An Aesop Fable

In expecting perfection, you have long set yourself up for certain failure (Messina). If your spouse expected it from you, then he was living in a dream world. If someone likes you, then you cannot do wrong and if not, then you cannot do right. If they do not want you, then it is strike three and you're out; if they do, then it is strike three and you are still in the game. *If you love somebody, let them go. If they return, they were always yours and if they don't, they never were. When others love us, they forgive even our crimes; when they do not love us, even our virtues go unappreciated,* says Honore de Balzac. You forgive people when they say that they are sorry and really mean it. If someone were as important to you as you were to them, then certainly you would not allow them to get away from you that readily.

Projection

"He was just up here and told me he was going to vote for me; now why would he double cross me?" asked a baffled Ralph Kramden when losing Joe Rumsey's vote for the Raccoon Lodge Convention Manager. If you remember this *Honeymooners* episode, the sudden change of heart was all over a faulty vacuum cleaner that Ralph had recommended to his lodge brother, a cause that he had never even considered.

They are sudden, shocking, painful, intense, nasty, bewildering and unpredictable. Since we were unable to read the other's mind, we wake up to the bitter reality that we did not know them as well as we had thought. We assume that they felt the same as we did and

The weather was getting cold. Hurrying to get into his warm house, a farmer saw a snake lying across the path. The farmer had compassion on the snake and he picked the snake up and put it under his cloak. He carried it down into the valley and laid it upon the ground. As the snake began to warm, he began o slither and move. He coiled up and struck, biting the farmer in the leg.

An old Fable

wanted what we wanted, and we are even convinced of our own erroneous conclusions. "If only I were nicer!" You might have been too nice, too giving and too gentle. Admitted Jennifer Lopez, "I just wanted to see what it was like to be a newlywed." Did her husband marry her for the same reason? "I just wanted to see what it was like to be married," Brittany Spears told *ET.* When was she going to let Jason Alexander in on it?

Prejudice sees only what it wants to see and not what is obvious, says Aubrey T. de Vere (Spanoudis). We color the world with projection–with our own thoughts, motives and assumptions, displacing onto others attitudes that we alone harbor (Willford). We see our faces in the mirror and our thoughts in the minds of others (Proverbs). We make assumptions (Messina). Dreams are in and of themselves episodes of projection. The thoughts and actions of each character and object as well as the character and object themselves are ours and us alone. We bring the figures to life. In those dreams in which we are feeding an ongoing movie or television program, we are as puppeteers, awaiting further plans and roles for the players. The friend who does something violent out of anger or frustration is actually a reflection of your own hostility. The character himself is lifeless. *Your* relationship and the cause of its demise was a presumption based on *your* reasoning, *your* rationale and *your* expectations. Other people do not always think, behave and react in accordance with our predictions and expectations. Some people operate out of a pattern of logic outside of the norm while others do not act out of logic or reason at all.

Getting out of Your Head–And into Theirs

The battle is not always to the strong, but time and chance happen to them all (The Preacher 9:11). We see "mismatches" all the time. There were infinite possibilities why she fled, and it may have had nothing to do with you even if she said it did. We interpret poems and paintings differently from other readers and observers, and we are often the victims of petty misunderstandings and disagreements. "Well, I thought you meant…" Alan Alda once said that our assumptions are our windows on the world. The inferences and conclusions that you draw are based on your projections, and what you project is what *you* think, what you would do if you were them. We interpret their actions and behaviors based on our own logic, values, morals, motives and experiences. What you speculated that they did out of benevolence might not have been anything less than an act of selfishness or deceit.

Do not let timeworn stereotypes and popular opinion blind you to reality. All that glitters is not gold. Many girls do just want to have fun. Real men do eat quiche. Daiquiris are not only for women, and straight bourbon is not only for men. "Only *men* use women for sex—it is more meaningful to a woman." Males can be sensitive too, and boys will not always be boys. In fact, research shows that it is men, ironically, who are prone to suffer more from the loss of love than women. Ask a mail deliverer if a dog is a man's best friend.

There are questions that simply cannot be answered. Indeed, the answers to your many questions may forever remain an unsolved mystery. The mind is far too complex to be deciphered or taken personally. People are so vastly different from one another that the odds of your speculation about why they left being correct are highly unlikely. Draw closure to your past by embracing your future.

How well did you know your lover? Perhaps you were unaware of the irreparable ramifications of her past. If your girlfriend lost her mother at the impressionable young age of five, for example, or if your boyfriend was the unfortunate victim of child abuse, then s/he may be sentenced to a lifetime of psychological obsessions, compulsions and predispositions, especially if these problems go untreated. Rituals, disorders, emotional or physical spouse abuse, intentional heartbreaking and problems with intimacy mask a childhood that may have been wrought with trauma, rejection, resentment and loss. Your physical or sexual aggressor may have been physically abused by his father or unloved by his mother and was harboring intense, deep-seated rage and hostility toward all men or women, and you might have simply been in the wrong place, at the wrong time and with the wrong person. They may have lost a parent during childhood and were fearful of abandonment. Your intentional heartbreaker may have been abused, sexually assaulted or witnessed a parent being battered and molested and was knowingly or unconsciously setting you up for disaster all the time. They had contempt for all men and women, and you happened to be in harm's way. A neglected or unloved child could not learn how to love; thus, it would be unlikely that she could love you or others. Your Casanova needed you and an endless number of other partners such as yourself to compensate for the love that he might not have received from his mother even as early as infancy. A faultfinder is going to leave you and others such as yourself for your failure to live up to the image of the perfect man or woman if she or he had no parents or appropriate role models on which to base his dreams and expectations. A young child who was forsaken by a parent is going to have trust issues in adulthood. An unloved, parentless, forgotten or abused child will have difficulty maintaining healthy relationships. Suppressed emotional memories will eventually be triggered at some point, unleashing years of pain and sadness. Your love for the victim who abandoned you might have brought to the surface many deep-rooted and painful feelings, and she might not have been able to handle the love and intimacy that you had to offer. Such a person is bound to begin and end promising relationships that grow, keep others at arm's length or sustain unloving and user-type arrangements. For them, this is preferable to reliving agonizing moments from childhood. *No amount of love in the present can assuage the pain of abandonment from the past,* says Geneen Roth in *When Food is Love*; one *can only allow oneself to feel the pain fully and release it in the present* (Primal Page).

Fragile: Handle with Care

It is an injustice to have to walk on eggshells all the time, worrying about offending someone, losing them and being judged by them. If you have been endlessly berating yourself because you should not have said this and maybe you should have done that, stop. It is unproductive and will only intensify and prolong your depression. Husbands and wives see each other at their absolute worst, but the two of them would never dream of living their lives apart from the other even though they get on each other's nerves at times. They bicker and then put it behind them. If you are *not* fighting, then something is wrong. *One who judges bears no reflection on you but reveals himself as one who needs to judge,* says author Wayne Dyer. Your judge, however, in judging you and others, is also perpetuating a chronic, life-long, self-judgmental disposition equal in reason and magnitude. *You can please some of the people some of the time, and most of the people most of the time, but you cannot please all of the people all of the time* said Abraham Lincoln. This is why a personal sense of self-worth is vital. You must appreciate who you are. We cannot continuously live our lives dedicated to the satisfaction of other people, and if those whom you cannot please insist on criticizing and condemning you, then they are not people whom you should want in your life anyway.

The ancient Chinese philosopher Confucius, as wise, enlightened, compassionate and educated as he was, was prone to fits of anger and infantile tit for tats. "Once," cites author Russell Freedman, "a character named Ru Bei sent a messenger to Confucius's home, asking for a meeting. Confucius disapproved of Ru Bei and wanted him to know it. He declined the meeting on the ground that he was ill. Then, as the messenger was going out the door, the wily philosopher took up his lute and began to sing loudly, making sure that he was heard. Another time, a rude and disrespectful youth incited Confucius to lose his temper. He gave the insolent young man a tongue lashing, then raised his walking stick and cracked the fellow across the shins" (Freedman 6-8). Christ not only went on a rampage in the holy temple that was being used as a place of business (Jn. 2:13), but He also cursed a fig tree for its failure to produce figs (Mk. 11:12).

Pearls before Swine

It is impossible to forgive yourself if all you do is lash yourself for everything that you do wrong and remain oblivious to all that you do right. For every vice within you there is also a virtue. The quarreler is also a fighter–passionate, determined, feisty, tenacious and devoted.

Were your tears considered a sign of weakness? Only a sensitive person could be full of love, compassion and empathy for others, despite the sadness or rage that comes with the package.

She said that you were too busy at the office? Who would not want a hustler who would work tooth and nail to provide his family with the best?

She claimed that you were too young for her? She will wish that she had a functional man of sixty when she is in her seventies. He thought that you were too old for him? He will appreciate your age-old wisdom and experience when he has dated naive and unsophisticated women.

You were outcast for your religious convictions? We should all be as fortunate for having that kind of faith.

They accused you of being too "clingy"? Why would someone prefer to live with the insecurity of having someone who might abandon them eventually?

Did you lavish her with love and affection? Were you nurturing, supportive, understanding, faithful, honest, sincere, thoughtful and considerate?

You praised him, made her feel special and tried to please her sexually.

He lost a woman who really cared and who would have given anything.

You were compromising and willing to make sacrifices. You went out of your way and drove long distances to see her.

You were giving. You showered him with thoughtful gifts. You sent flowers and other thoughtful gifts to her job. You remembered his birthday and other special occasions, sending cards and gifts.

You wined her and dined her, took her places and broadened her horizons.

You were fun to be around, easy to talk to and get along with.

You were helpful.

You tried to entertain her with your sense of humor.

Most women would have appreciated your chivalry, the gentlemanly way you helped them on with their coat, sat them at the table and opened the door for them, and if you gallantly put yourself in harm's way to defend her or him, then you were indeed one of a dying breed. It was a lucky man who had a woman with your ladylike manners and your gracefulness.

A good wife is more precious than jewels (Pr. 31:10). He should have been grateful having a woman of virtue. She should have boasted of your principle and moral. Your integrity, sincerity, tenacity, determination, spunk, passion and drive were qualities to be admired.

You were to be respected for your political convictions and your patriotic zeal.

He should have been elated to have a woman who was genuine, unpretentious, down-to-earth, spiritual, virtuous and altruistic.

She had a man who was well-rounded, multifaceted and accomplished. He should have boasted of your knowledge and wisdom.

He should have beamed with pride over his Ivy League graduate, his brilliant Ph.D., his clever attorney, his intelligent physician and his creative artist. He had a responsible executive, a devoted secretary. A woman would have marveled at her skillful aviator, her creative educator, her talented performer, her courageous police officer or her heroic firefighter. She should have complimented you on your fine taste, well-groomed appearance and your good looks. Your interests, passions, skills, talents and abilities should have fascinated her. Your athletic prowess was overlooked. Our best blessings are often the least appreciated. You were not appreciated for who you are and what you did. Your critic and faultfinder may look back and appreciate the very things that they condemned you for while you are looking back with contempt for *their* faults and eccentricities.

Choose to acknowledge and appreciate all of your attributes and all that you contributed during the relationship. We are our own

Two Travelers, walking in the noonday sun, sought the shade of a wide spreading tree to rest. As they lay looking up among the pleasant leaves, they saw that it was a Plane tree. "How useless is the Plane!" said one of them. "It bears no fruit, and only serves to litter the ground with leaves." "Ungrateful creatures!" said a voice from the Plane Tree. "You lie here in my cooling shade, and yet you say that I am useless! Thus ungratefully do men receive their blessings!"

    Aesop

worst critics, wallowing in self-annihilation, and are inclined to greatly exaggerate our own shortcomings and imperfections.

In expecting the impossible from ourselves, living for and striving to please others, we do not allow ourselves to evolve. Mistakes are inevitable. Perfection can only theoretically be achieved through a lifetime of mistakes and imperfections, for it is failure that educates and improves us.

Accepting ourselves for whom and what we are absolves us of our ominous demand and expectation for perfection. For many of us, our inability and unwillingness to accept disownment by our parents unendingly compels us to maintain the illusion that the fault lies solely within us and that it is still not too late to win their love if only we had cut our hair, became a doctor, married the right person, earned more money or called home more often.

According to psychoanalyst John Staton, we compulsively seek reasons to blame ourselves in an effort to rationalize or justify their actions. Consider the following diagram:

We tend to fill in the blanks and see complete pictures even when small parts are missing. This is especially true when the object depicted is familiar. Dotted and dashed lines, for example, can substitute for complete lines. The mind's tendency toward closure, even if self-recriminating, naturally compels us to draw conclusions, especially when the only precedents that we have to work with are recorded mental tapes of guilt, blame and shame. Being our own harsh critics, we have assumed and are perfectly willing to accept culpability for the allegations and decisions of other people. In addition, feeling at fault for negative circumstances that have befallen you or others, feelings of 'regret' for real or 'imagined' misdeeds, a 'sense of remorse for unacceptable thoughts, feelings or attitudes,' loss and shame for not having done or said something to someone who is no longer available to you and a strong moral sense of right and wrong that inhibits you from choosing a "wrong" course of action can all generate guilt (Buss 111-16). We blame ourselves for falling short of our own familial and societal-based acquired standards of perfection and right and wrong, expectations that are no better lived up to by the authorities who dictated them.

It happens. We neither know what happened nor why, nor might we ever know. It is not our task to solve this mystery, however. We cannot penetrate the minds of other people. *Most of our assumptions have outlived their uselessness*, points out Marshall McLuhan, and any supposition that you might deduce would be nothing more than a projection of your own values, logic and reasoning.

Why J or K Became X?

- *He was intimidated by your intelligence.*

- *You were not intelligent enough for him.*

- *You called his/her marriage bluff.*

- *She was through using you.*

- *She discovered that she was latent.*

- *She was confused.*

- *You smoked.*

Why J or K Became X?

- *You didn't smoke.*

- *You were not handsome enough.*

- *She was threatened by your good looks.*

- *Being seen with someone small made them feel insecure.*

- *Being with someone tall made them feel insecure.*

- *Being with someone older made him/her uncomfortable.*

- *Being with someone younger made him/her uncomfortable*

- *Her age started to show.*

- *She preferred her own kind.*

- *She preferred Italians.*

- *He preferred blondes.*

- *He preferred brunettes.*

- *The two of you were too different.*

- *The two of you were too similar.*

In a survey conducted among several abandonment victims, it was found that 9 out of 10 persons who had abandoned their partners shared most of the following common personality and behavior traits (Sylvia):

- *selfish*
- *untrustworthy*
- *jealous*
- *possessive*
- *emotionally abusive*
- *physically abusive*
- *arrogant*
- *egocentric*
- *manipulative*
- *two*-faced

THE DR. JEKYLL/ MR. HYDE SYNDROME

While most recipients of heartbreak reported most of the above personality traits of their former lovers, all reported that their former lovers were very loving initially until the end when they suddenly pulled a complete 180-degree mysterious behavior shift. What accounts for this dichotomy?

The duality of man is the theme of Robert Louis Stevenson's *Dr. Jekyll and Mr. Hyde.* Jekyll, a prominent English scientist who has had to repress a lifetime of hostility for namesake, attempts to purge the evil side of his human nature through the ingestion of a self-created substance. The drug, however, seduces his hideous, evil, lustful and murderous Mr. Hyde side beyond his ability or willingness to control it—he delights in his evil (Wiley).

The Dr. Jekyll/Mr. Hyde syndrome refers to one who has *quasi-schizophrenic*, alternating phases of pleasantness and un-pleasantness; between charming and extremely unpleasant behavior. An individual's continuing pattern of lifelong repression of his dark side due to familial and societal expectations and restrictions may manifest itself as hostility and hatred toward the other person in

THE CURSE OF MANKIND SEEMED TO BE THAT MAN SHOULD HAVE TWO SEPARATE NATURES WITHIN HIMSELF.
DR. JEKYLL

the relationship after an extended facade of pleasantness and contentment (Wiley). Your former spouse or partner may have had pent up anger and resentment from early on, and because of her inability to express it properly, it came on strongly and suddenly by perhaps something as insignificant as a topless tube of toothpaste.

Conscientiousness and Guilt

One endures sorrows while suffering unjustly (1 Pet. 2:19-21). Sincerity can be a dangerous quality, especially when it is surrounded by deceit and impurity. It is the cross of the conscientious to endure sorrows, the burden of the mindful to suffer unjustly and the curse of the sensitive to bear the crosses, burdens and sufferings of unscrupulous partners and others who exploit the good-natured and use their conscientiousness against their favor (Piper 92). It is both a curse and a blessing, for it is the mindful who strive, the conscientious who win favor and the sensitive who show compassion.

Do You See What I See?

"Is that what all of the fuss was about?" you would be likely to say had you known what their reason for leaving really was. It usually has very little to do with what you imagine to be the culprit from your end. People are generally more forgiving than we think, and self-perception can be astronomically different from others' perception of us; thus, what you imagined to be of paramount ado may have been of little significance to him. What seemed a mountain to you might have been a molehill to her (Baker).

Repression, Resistance, & Denial

Guilt may have some of its roots in repression, resistance and denial (Baker). Sigmund Freud addressed the concept of *repression* to a forum of psychiatrists by liking it to a disruptive audience member who must be kept inside of a room away from the assembly and its speaker who are trying to stay mindful of his presentation. The defiant spectator, however, in a noisy charade, attempting to free himself of his incarceration, necessitates four personnel to keep the door closed, hence, repressed. Similarly, when we deny and repress painful feelings, we are merely putting a lid on a force that cannot be ignored. These feelings must be experienced, confronted and dealt with (Messina). *Full acceptance living* requires one to be fully open to the experience rather than in *denial* or *resistance* (Lozoff). The only way out is through.

Nobody savors criticism from others; even constructive criticism is difficult to hear, but even more intolerable and unbearable than this are self-assessment and self-critique. They humble us and force us to admit to ourselves that we are not without flaw, as if being less than perfect was a sin or crime to which we alone are not excused. As a result of this, we successfully repress, deny, rationalize and make excuses rather than take an honest look at ourselves and determine what needs to be done.

Repression and *avoidance* foster distorted and erroneous thinking and association, including guilt. Lyman Baker illustrated this mental split with a story of two sisters, one of whom lost the other to a tragic illness. The surviving sibling, having had affectionate feelings for the latter's husband, associated her sister's death with her secret desire for her brother-in-law, thus precipitating a superstitious form of guilt. This naturally intensified her grief. Situations of mental conflict are exceedingly common, Baker maintains, and efforts to ward off painful memories are quite regularly to be observed without their producing the result of a mental split. This division of the personality into a conscious and unconscious domain results in a disguised substitute for the repressed feelings that are unacceptable to the person's conscious conception of himself. If what was repressed is brought back again into conscious mental activity with the help of a therapist, then the resulting psychical conflict that the patient had tried to avoid can reach a better outcome than was offered by repression. Then will dissociation occur. Baker's story serves as a model to demonstrate how self-imposed, erroneous guilt can arise from an abandonment as a result of undesirable thoughts, attitudes, actions and situations that may have transpired during two individuals' time together. "I'm to blame!" "If only I hadn't wished him harm!" "God punished me!"

Guilty of the Womb

Webster's defines guilt as *feelings of culpability for imagined offences or from a sense of inadequacy.* It is something that is generally attributed to acts of crime, violations of law and breach of conduct (Merriam-Webster Collegiate Dictionary 11: 555). Feeling guilt and shameful for relatively trivial things that you might have said or done during the relationship is irrational. Just because you feel guilty does not mean that you are, or does it necessarily have anything to do with the termination of your relationship. Guilt has its origin in perfectionism (Messina). It is irrational to insist that you be perfect. Certainly the people in your life who instilled this idea in your head were not perfect. We all make mistakes. It is part of being human. As long as you continue to focus on your flaws, then you shall continue to set yourself up for failure by expecting yourself to live up to self-imposed, impossible standards. Bertrand Russell put it perfectly when he said that fools and fanatics are always so certain of themselves but wiser people so full of doubts.

You have the right and privilege of being imperfect. You are entitled to be angry. It is your prerogative to yell, curse and complain. You have the right to all of these things—as does everybody else. When the prophets told us to be perfect, they were speaking more in the context of striving rather than achieving. They knew that they were expecting the impossible. I am willing to bet that the person who hurt you capitalized on your guilt and need for perfection to induce you into justifying their disappearing act at the end. You may be blind to it at the moment, but in time you will realize that she was not the innocent babe of the woods, and he was not Prince Charming.

As perfectionists, we are inherently prone to guilt and depression. Self-esteem and self-confidence are uphill battles for us.

I can find no evidence of the kind of the Christ people seem to have invented and created. There is no evidence of Christ, meek and mild. I can find Christ the compassionate, the gentle, but I also find a very temperamental, aggressive, passionate and often angry man a lot of the time.

Actor Robert Powell of *Jesus of Nazareth (Re Jesus)*

We cannot accept in ourselves anything less than optimum behavior and performance, and when we fall short of these impossible expectations, shame, discouragement and depression arise (Messina). As children, we might have felt pressured to overachieve for one reason or another, and guilt might have been employed by our parents or educators to control and manipulate us. It is much easier to regulate children who are conscientious, eager to please and afraid to disappoint than those who are rebellious. As adults, we found people such as our family and authority figures who repeated this mind game with us, capitalizing on our perfectionism and eagerness to please, using our guilt and shame to their advantage during the relationship and using it against us after they had decided to dissolve it. It should come as no mystery, then, why we are left feeling devastated and culpable.

Guilt is likewise a motivator to falsely amend all of the self-perceived wrongs of which you were not guilty to begin with (Messina). It subconsciously propels you to be better than you already are. What may be felt and interpreted as guilt might actually be feelings of an impending low self-esteem, which has undoubtedly taken an abysmal plunge after recent circumstances.

Self-Esteem

A person devotes endless days and nights completing a major project, and we tell him that he is obsessive. She lives for her job and for her children in the classroom, and her colleagues gossip that she has no life. Her determination is considered aggression. The "virile" consider sensitive men weak or effeminate. You had the principle and boldness to stand up for your woman and yourself, and she complained that you were too confrontational. Your eager response to your second grade teacher's "open-ended" question was unusually profound, and she humiliated you for being "out in left field." You invested your heart, soul and savings into endeavoring onto your career, while your friends and peers were putting theirs into parties and beer, yet your parents criticized you for wasting your money on a foolish dream. You were willing to make moves, take risks and try different things; however, they said that you were being ludicrous. You had the courage and the right to confront your former spouse for the damage that s/he caused, but in the eyes of the law you were stalking them. That rigid accountant whom you married condemned you for your creativity, wondering how he could have gotten involved with someone "weird." Dad fails to notice your impeccable suit, but he is the first to inform you that your tie is too loose. *While we are indifferent to our good qualities, we keep on deceiving ourselves in regard to our faults, until we come to look at them as virtues*, said Heinrich Heine.

You alone must acknowledge and take pride in yourself. We cannot be expected to feel good about our attributes if we leave them in the hands of the people in our lives who may fail to recognize them. If the only things that are broadcast are our imperfections, then we cannot realize our blessings. If we are constantly bombarded with complaints, criticisms and accusations, then it is no wonder why we internalize the actions of the person who hurt us. Cease the guilt-driven need for perfection. If only your former lover were as conscientious as yourself. It is your conscientiousness that is perpetuating your guilt and your conscientiousness that was used against you. You let your conscience be their guide.

CHARACTER

People can be heartless, can't they? Consider the kind of person with whom you were dealing. Did she keep any sort of amicable relationship with her divorcee? Abraham Lincoln said that character is like a tree and reputation like its shadow. The shadow is what we think of it; the tree is the real thing. We all get miffed and peeved over annoyances and inconveniences, but perhaps they were excessive about it.

Every good tree produces fine fruit, but every rotten tree produces worthless fruit (Mt. 7:17). Would those who knew her say that she had a good heart and that she was a nice, caring person and a pleasure to be around (Pearsall 27-28)?

For over twenty years, I have had the opportunity to work with twelve-year-old children, their siblings and their parents and have observed the following traits typical of those with one or more types of personality disorders. The description that follows is meant to relieve you of what might perhaps be a very heavy burden that you have been carrying on your shoulders, thinking that you were responsible for what might have been erratic and unwarranted behavior on the part of your lover:

- *Denial of having caused misery or harm*

The greatest of faults is to be conscious of none, wrote Thomas Carlyle. Individuals with personality disorders will not own up to the responsibility or blame for having hurt another person or having done them wrong, and if one actually succeeds in eliciting an apology out of one of them, then he is a rare sort indeed (Metcalf). Being unable to admit to imperfection, they will always justify themselves with excuses and rationalizations and cast responsibility and culpability onto others, namely those whom they have hurt. In very extreme cases, they may actually have no recollection of having caused misery or harm at all (Home Data West). Many have no regard for the feelings or rights of other people or the harm that they bring (Tiscali). They can be tactless, aggressive, insensitive, offensive and bullish without any moral or conscientious regard for the people whom they hurt and the lives that they destroy (Angel). They mask their deeply embedded insecurity and trivial minds with an outer persona of conceit, affectedness and exaggerated self-importance (World Book, Inc.). *Beware of the adulterer and adulteress whose lips drip with honey and whose mouth is smoother than oil; but in the end are as bitter as wormwood and as sharp as a two-edged sword* (Pr. 5:3-4).

- ## *Excessive grudge holding*

  Life is an adventure in forgiveness, quoted Gandhi, and it takes a wise and virtuous mind to be able to pardon another for the physical or emotional harm that he inflicts. People suffering from mood disorders have difficulty forgiving others and may impose an extended silent treatment or cold shoulder even for what would normally be regarded as a trivial matter; thus, they will end long-time relationships and marriages out of obstinacy (Tiscali; World Book, Inc.).

- ## *Frequent contradiction of self and others*

  Those with mental disorders are inconsistent and illogical, often making flippant and discrepant assertions (Metcalf). Many of them are compulsive liars and will state arguments supporting opinions or allegations even if both are knowingly erroneous (World Book, Inc.).

- ## *Frequent mood swings*

  They have split personalities, smiles one moment and your worst enemy the next, and over something that you would never have imagined (Home Data West). They tend to blow things way out of proportion (Tiscali; World Book, Inc.). Cease second guessing yourself and trying to turn back the clock and do it all differently. You cannot predict or prevent these occurrences from individuals with personality disorders. They are inevitable.

- ## *Critical*

  H.L. Mencken once said that a cynic is a man who, when he smells flowers, looks around for a coffin. Your character is also your fate. You need only observe the people with whom one associates to determine this truth for yourself. Many people with emotional disorders are chronic complainers, always judgmental and unable to acknowledge or appreciate the attributes and sincerity in others (Metcalf; World Book, Inc.). They know the price of everything, said Oscar Wilde, and the value of nothing, focusing in on every fault but never paying you a compliment or word of gratitude (Home Data West). Instead of thanking her for the thoughtful gift that she had brought back for him from vacation, Willy told Sorry that the present was impractical. My ex was very quick to highlight my flaws. You could never have satisfied, pleased or made your former mate happy if he or she was a critic. They would have, however, continued to make you unhappy, bringing you down into their pit of doom and negativity. It seemed as if the harder that Sonny tried to please Mona with his $150 dinners and sterling silver jewelry, the less appreciative that she was, always making reference to others who would have done more. Grace, on the other hand, could not thank Ben enough for the simplest gestures. It is easy to be critical; it is far more difficult to attempt what others criticize you for attempting. Gratitude is the parent of and greatest of all virtues said Cicero; thus, one who cannot appreciate beneficence leaves much to be desired.

• *Paranoid*

Persons with one or more antisocial personality disorders may be suspicious of the good intentions of others (World Book, Inc.). Feeling victimized themselves by the cold, cruel world out there, they are frequently on the defensive and may believe that their former partner was "out to get them" and "struck first before the iron got hot" (Home Data West). "That was just a last minute bargaining chip," Kathy told Pat when he promised to give her the house and the child that she claimed she had wanted, discounting all gestures of sincerity.

• *Controlling*

"Do it my way!" they insist. Individuals with severe obsessive disorders have an excessive need for control (World Book, Inc.).

They may be excessive planners and prepared with a system for everything that they do (Metcalf). Organization and cleanliness are certainly desirable qualities, and perhaps cultural, but not when they become inordinate and dominate our lives.

- *Pretentious*

My son, may you call understanding itself 'Kinswoman,' to guard you against the stranger and the cunning of heart, who says, I have come out to meet you, to look for your face, that I may find you, cautioned King Solomon to his son (*New World Translation of the Holy Scriptures* 844-45). *They will mislead you by the abundance of their persuasiveness and by the smoothness of their lips will they seduce you, until an arrow cleaves open your liver,* he goes on to warn him. *They will lure you with their charm and promises.* They can also be callous and cold, except when their act requires a sympathetic countenance; thus, their acts of sincerity and compassion are nothing more than facades (Home Data West). Many do not have the ability to experience the full range of human emotion and are unable to sympathize with another's suffering (Metcalf). Others have learned to suppress their feelings, perhaps out of self-preservation (World Book, Inc.).

Nobody's Fault?

Ron was happily married for fifteen years with three children, and his wife left him one day for a retiring police officer. Her new husband has threatened Ron on more than one occasion, and his former wife denies him visitation rights to his son and daughter. One woman's husband insisted that she abort a child that they would have had together only to divorce her and have a child with someone else. Now she is no longer able to bear children. Another man divorced his wife because she put in long hours at work and was always tired. Paul intends to end his relationship with Mary, so why is he making plans with her for New Years Eve?

Disloyalty and abandonment are not only relegated to loving partnerships. We hear of adult children abandoning their parents or behaving as vultures, fighting over inheritances. People generally hurt others for the following reasons:

• *To justify their position*

She tried vainly to start an argument and incite him so that she could convince herself and others that she had made the right choice by ending their relationship. When her attempt failed, she resorted to cruel and unwarranted behavior. This woman was to be his wife only months earlier. Some people would rather bring harm and suffering to other people by their accusations, rather than spare those endless years of needless guilt and suffering, instead of being frank. Their honesty, of course, would be self-incriminating, exposing their true motives.

• *Genetics*

There are a number of individuals in the world who are inherently predisposed to hurtful and destructive behavior. They are indiscriminate in their disposition, hating anyone whom they encounter without just cause or reason. They occupy our prisons, violent wards and unfortunately, our hearts. Genes indeed play a major role in aggressive or abusive behavior. The apple doesn't fall far from the tree. Just ask any teacher after a parent/teacher conference.

• *They enjoy it*

Before she left, Sadie intentionally hurt Angela with some cruel remarks, knowing that they would cut right to the core, deriving pleasure in her cruelty. This had been an existing pattern of behavior even prior to their relationship. There are those who obtain gratification through the infliction of physical or mental pain onto others. The person who hurt you might have actually taken pleasure and satisfaction in your pain and tears. Did they abandon you when you were down, or did they support and stand by you when you needed them by your side? Although you might be unable or unwilling to acknowledge and admit it to yourself right now, perhaps your former partner exhibited even the most subtle signs of sadistic behavior throughout the relationship toward you and other people.

• *Control*

Narcissists, power seekers, bullies and other insecure people try to hurt others as a means of control and defense of their security. They are extremely insecure and tend to knock and discourage those who are "up." The breakup might have been the pre-plotted finale of a relationship based on the fulfillment of control, and it was now time for the closing curtain.

• *Unhappiness*

Hurt people hurt people, according to author Sandy Wilson. Misery begets misery. We give to the world what we receive. The outside reflects the inside. Whatever it was that was done to you might have actually been done to him by a significant figure in his life. Those who have experienced childhood abuse may compulsively and perpetually displace their repressed hostility onto substitute objects, namely those around them. Your former boyfriend or girlfriend, for example, may have experienced a very painful childhood wrought with abuse and neglect and was passing on to you the legacy passed down to him. Hurtful behavior is not always willed, however, as much of these childhood traumas occur during what Freud termed the *latency period*, in which estrangement of earliest memories and facts that we find evil are repressed into the preconscious (Felluga). That which is withheld is in and of itself divulging.

A Pardon from the Warden

Let him among you who is without sin cast the first stone, retorted Christ to the lynching mob (Jn. 8:7). The paralytic in the *New Testament* was metaphorically paralyzed with guilt rather than the commonly held belief that he was paralyzed of the body (Rifkin). Christ's absolution of the man's sins is what freed him of his affliction (*Holy Bible* 859). Certainly you did not commit so heinous a deed to warrant such pain and suffering. *Take heart, for your sins are forgiven* (Mt. 9:2), and stop apologizing for your infirmities. You are a human being with faults, as was your lover. Do not justify their decision or make excuses for them. You may have fallen victim to criticism and blame all of your life. Also, do not look to them for validation; you will fall short.

I'm OK You're OK
The Proof Is in the Pudding

Striving in vain to live up to your own and others' standards of perfection for acceptance and approval is a serious impediment toward growth and self-esteem (Messina). Many of psychologist Dennis Jaffe's patients have experienced a neglect of their most basic, deepest human needs–for touching and for companionship; for sharing inner feelings; for expressing creative energy; for sexual fulfillment; for personal validation and for the giving and receiving of love. Instead, their lives were characterized by duty and obligation to the very people who gave them little or nothing in return (Primal Page). Growing up enveloped in a world of negativity, coupled with a critical, abusive and non-nurturing significant other, can wreak havoc on your feelings of self-worth and self-acceptance. The experience has opened up an emotional can of worms that had held a tight lid for too long. It was a matter of time and experience before it would pop open. Time was loosening it. If not this, then it would have been something else. Your pain attests to your love, and an ability to love reflects an ability to *be* loved. Remorse is proof of conscientiousness, and sorrow affirms your sincerity. Intense feelings are a tribute to your emotional well-being and agility. If you cannot feel, then you cannot heal. Through belief in yourself, accomplishment, positive feedback and some pampering, you can reverse this trend.

Conditional Love

A relationship can make you or break you, and if "I love you–as long as..." was the implied stipulation, then it is of little mystery why you were sentenced to an unmitigated depressive episode and abysmal self-esteem, undoubtedly spawned by their conditional love and insidiously in pursuit until it finally caught up. Conditional love is not love; it is merely control and dominance. *Love me when I least deserve it,* says an old Swedish proverb, *because that's when I really need it.* If you were loved with loopholes, then you did not receive a just deserter, and the only error in judgment here is your own; thus, your fruitless hopes and dreams to win the unconditional love, respect, approval and admiration of a conditionally loving, disrespectful, disapproving and unappreciative recipient, as a hamster running on a circular treadmill, is only perpetuating a delusional fantasy that could never come to fruition. By misdirecting your personal tribute away from yourself, the person who should receive and acknowledge the fruits of your tree, and in fantasy, directing them toward she or he who would only reject them, you are preventing yourself from reaping all that you have sown and continuing to destroy whatever self-esteem that was not destroyed in the relationship.

It's Their Loss

A good wife lost, is God's gift lost said Benjamin Franklin. You hear sob stories and horror tales about the "creeps," "weirdos" and "losers" out there and you ask, "What more do they want?" "She lost a good man!" "He lost a loving woman!" "She didn't deserve you!" "He was lucky to have you!" Accentuate your sincerity and goodness. Appreciate your attributes and your assets. Acknowledge all that you have done and contributed. You had much to offer. *A successful marriage requires falling in love many times, always with the same person,* emphasized Mignon McLaughlin. Some individuals have to meet the wrong people a few times before they appreciate what they have lost. Just recall the men and women in your past who would have sacrificed their right arm to have what you offer, who would have appreciated how lucky they were to have you and who would have settled for less than what you gave the individual who hurt you. Your loving efforts were in vain with this one. So do not sell yourself short. There really is better out there waiting for you to recover.

It's Nothing Personal.

A critic's comments and actions are a *projection* or *transference* of her own issues. Other people's behavior makes more of a statement about themselves than it does about you (FitzMaurice). Criticism is in their nature. Look around your personal circle. If they have criticized you, then they were undoubtedly bound to have criticized and judged others as well.

ALL YOUR FAULT
POINTING THE FINGER

Look Where It's Coming From

You cannot expect sympathy from the unsympathetic, love from a narcissist and sincerity from the superficial. If they were inconsiderate of your feelings during the relationship, then you need not be shocked that they let you down so insensitively at the end. Do not assume that you can win over someone spoiled, and do not seek the truth from a liar or faithfulness from the unfaithful. Acceptance from the intolerant and compliments from a critic are likewise futile attempts.

Freud's *ego-ideal* explains why people tend to have this delusion of grandeur, expecting the utopian from others even when others are unable to live up to the ideal. According to Freud, the *ego-ideal* is the precipitate of the old picture of parents–the expression for the perfection that the child attributed to them. We expect others to live up to the standards of perfection, which we erroneously credited our parents, and when we get an incongruent response, then we are left dumbfounded, disbelieving even the obvious. The picture perfect world stems from Lacan's *ego-ideal theory*, asserting that our glorified perception of the world around us emanates from the mirror-perfect image that we observed of ourselves from as early as 6 to 18 months of age (Felluga).

ACTIONS SPEAK LOUDER THAN WORDS

We all speak ill and fall short of expectations. Certainly your emotions may have gotten the best of you sometimes. Perhaps you may have been reluctant to do something difficult, but when push came to shove did you deliver? If you were sincere, faithful and did your best to make her happy and to make things special for him, then stop shining the spotlight on your undesirable traits, and cease assuming that it was something that you did or said even if they said it was. Two to one, half a dozen or the other, they say. If it was not the topless toothpaste, then it would have been the socks on the floor. They would have found something else to complain about. People who love each other do not leave each other. Instead of focusing on all of the "bad" things that you did and the "wonderful" things that they did, think about all of the bad things that they did and the wonderful things that you did. Do you try to do the right thing? Have a little faith in yourself. You have a heart and a conscience. If this were not true, then you would not be in this much pain. Truly abhorrent people do not have consciences; that is why they can live selfish lives hurting people repeatedly. They operate out of anger, hostility, jealousy and resentment.

Chapter Summary

Self-esteem suffers in the aftermath of a loss by a significant other, generating guilt and shame. In addition, an unhealthy relationship with a critical and unnurturing person gradually erodes our self-image, again, producing guilt as a result (Messina). The mind's compunction for rationalization and closure likewise finds its answers in a barrage of blame and self-deprecation, and if you were held culpable for losses and mishaps in your early past or for failure to live up to a code of perfection and divinity, then sole accountability or remorse is likely to arise as an emotional by-product (Staton). *We are often of greater importance in our own eyes than in the eyes of our neighbor* preached Aesop; hence, we feel surprised and offended when we are spurned by others who do not share the same significant perception that we hold for ourselves. Liking yourself comes first. Repairing damaged self-confidence is crucial toward abandonment recovery, and this long and demanding task will eventually be effected through achievement and by meeting and overcoming challenges and obstacles that we encounter.

One cannot hammer a mountainous-sized groove or puncture into the exterior of the universe without repercussions of proportionate magnitude. No act of kindness goes unnoticed, and no act of harm goes unpunished.

Put an end to the projecting. Quit blaming yourself. Stop praising her. Start praising yourself. You probably did more good than you recall, and they were not the saints whom you may have perceived them to be. Cease internalizing this, and refrain from measuring yourself against a phantom entity of perfection; otherwise, you shall continue to set yourself up for guilt and depression. You shall slip into an abysmal crevice of poor self-concept. Their love was a selfish love. If you were really that important, if they really cared and if they truly ever had any intention of keeping a relationship with you, then they would have.

Stop berating yourself for who you are not and what you do not offer, and start appreciating who you are and what you do have to give. That steadfast fighter of principle has been in your corner for many rounds now, keeping you from getting knocked down. It has made you a champion. That overly sensitive "effeminate" is what has enabled others to feel at ease and confide in you.

You might have fallen in love with an act, a lie. Not everyone with whom we get involved loves us. Many people get into relationships not out of sincere love but out of need, yet many of these false lovers are crafty in planting an illusion of love and sincerity in their partners. It is little surprise why the rejected partner is shocked and even traumatized when the deserting party suddenly and unexpectedly calls the whole thing off without any remorse or regard. To add insult to injury, they will come up with some feeble excuse, blaming the other for their decision. Remember, their behavior is about them and not you (FitzMaurice). Their rejection of you, their peeves, expectations and demands were also about them and not you. You are not center stage. Each of us is enveloped in our own chamber of emotions, life experiences, attitudes, opinions, prejudices and irrational thinking.

Who we are and what we do reveals our past (Primal Page). Recall the scars suffered by your unsympathetic spouse who was unloved, sexually assaulted, physically abused, abandoned or traumatized at an early age. Deep inside, he or she may still be that unfortunate eight-year-old child.

You hurt because you can love, and you take on the burden of guilt because of your conscientiousness. Not everyone will experience love in this lifetime, and not everyone will receive the full gamut of pain and pleasure. Be it a blessing or a curse in your own eyes, you are one of a chosen few. Those who can experience a very brief hurt and move onto the next have not or are not able to experience love. Your former partner, who could look you squarely in the eyes and say goodbye without remorse, may have been unable or unwilling to experience love and intimacy for various factors beyond his or her knowledge or understanding. Again, do not ascribe to obsolete notions regarding femininity or masculinity, for instance, the "Real men don't cry!" stereotype, for these are nothing more than generalizations. Men and women both suffer devastation.

Another man, woman, fickleness, a recent breakup among his or her family or friends, or whatever it might have been, you really do not know what happened, but it is unfair for you to expect yourself to live up to a double standard and assume fault. Consider the source, and do not personalize this. You were not the first, and you shall not be the last. Perhaps the only thing you are doing wrong is getting involved with the wrong people.

After he was carried across the stream by the Frog, the Scorpion stung him. "You promised you wouldn't sting me if I carried you across the stream," cried the Frog, "why have you done this to me?" The latter replied, "I am a Scorpion."
An old Fable

After returning from a walk in the forest, the little boy said to his grandfather, "Grandfather, the Hyena laughed at me, the Fox deceived me, the Lion roared at me and the Snake bit me. What did I do wrong?" he cried. "My dear boy," replied the old man, "hyenas laugh, foxes deceive, lions roar and snakes bite. The only thing you did wrong was go into the forest."

The Author

After a time, you may find that
"having" is not so
pleasing a thing, after all,
as "wanting." It is not
logical, but it is often true.

Leonard Nimoy

CHAPTER III
Be Thankful

CHAPTER III: Be Thankful

A Shepherd, counting his Sheep one day, discovered that a number of them were missing. Much irritated, he very loudly and boastfully declared that he would catch the thief and punish him as he deserved. The Shepherd suspected a Wolf of the deed and so set out toward a rocky region among the hills, where there were caves infested by Wolves. But before starting out he made a vow to Jupiter that if he would help him find the thief he would offer a fat Calf as a sacrifice. The Shepherd searched a long time without finding any Wolves, but just as he was passing near a large cave on the mountain side, a huge Lion stalked out, carrying a Sheep. In great terror the Shepherd fell on his knees. "Alas, O Jupiter, man does not know what he asks! To find the thief I offered to sacrifice a fat Calf. Now I promise you a full-grown Bull, if you but make the thief go away!"

An Aesop Fable

From Romance to Repulsion
Be Careful What You Wish For-You May "Get It"

He was so loving, so sweet! "She was an adorable little doll, my little angel!" "I'll never meet anyone like her again!" you weep incessantly. "I miss him so much!" "Will I ever hear from her again?"

I recall my first therapy session with John, some four months following my broken engagement, and how I was struck by the awe-inspiring way in which he could look at my situation from a positive, encouraging perspective, in dichotomous contrast to my own typical pattern of pessimism, reshaping and rebuilding my positive self-concept and outlook once again. It was as if I had been programmed all of my life to think from a negative perspective, and somebody outside of my familiar world of doom and gloom was now attempting to reprogram me or teach an old dog a new trick.

There is a Chinese folk tale about a farmer whose only horse had run away one day. The townspeople, after hearing about the loss, immediately rushed to the farmer's aid to offer their condolences. "Isn't it a terrible thing?" they commiserated, to which the farmer replied, "Maybe." The townspeople were very perplexed by the farmer's nonchalant response; they did not understand why losing his horse did not trouble him. Much time had elapsed, and the horse finally returned to the farmer, this time with several other horses. The townspeople were delighted when they heard the good news and wasted no time racing over to the farmer to offer their congratulations and share in his joy. "Isn't it a great thing?" they expressed with delight. The farmer again replied, "Maybe." Naturally the townspeople were surprised at his lack of joy. Some time later, the farmer's son upon riding one of the horses was thrown from the horse and broke his leg. Once again the townspeople rushed to the farmer to offer their condolences. Surely this man must be devastated, they thought. "Isn't it a terrible thing?" they asked, to which the farmer answered, "Maybe." Again they were puzzled. Why was he unmoved, they wondered? His son was injured. Well soon afterward, war had broken out, and every able-bodied young man was called to fight except for the farmer's son, of course, whose leg was broken falling off the horse.

The late author Peter McWilliams tried to impress upon us the repercussions of negative thinking on our psychological and physiological well-being in *You Can't Afford the Luxury of a Negative Thought*.

**You have played the harlot
with many lovers;
would you return to me?
Jeremiah 3:1**

Be careful what you set your heart upon, warned Ralph Waldo Emerson, *for you will surely have it*. Benjamin Franklin wrote that if one could have half of his wishes that he would double his troubles. In other words, you may get what you like, but then you may not like what you get or the subsequences of having acquired it. How often have you had your hopes and prayers answered only to regret it later? Bad things often lead to good things and vice versa. One thing always leads to another. Let the chips fall where they may. It takes two to tango. If it is meant to happen, then it will. Free yourself of despair. Liberate yourself from hope. Hope assumes a wish, a goal, a fabricated and predetermined outcome that disillusions us when we get it half the time anyway. We have all heard it a hundred times–"I'm sorry she came back to me!" "I'd rather be alone and depressed than have her back!" "This is not as good as I thought it would be!" If you have ever gone shopping, obsessed with finding this one item and one item only, later to discover something even better on the rack, something you had not planned on, then you have learned that, ironically, most of the greatest moments in your life come when you least expect it. You could find something on the rack tomorrow.

Chopped Liver

"Maybe he'll call me by the end of the week," you hope. "Perhaps I should call her," you think. I truly empathize with the overwhelming compulsion to telephone or pay a visit to the person who has abandoned you. You want to express your feelings, apologize and make amends. You are reluctant and hope that he or she will call you first. Friends advise against it. Although the probability of a change of heart is quite small, *one* telephone call, letter or e-mail might be advisable to release your feelings, attempt to make amends and bring closure. Any subsequent communication or attempt to save the relationship is an exercise in futility and strongly inadvisable. Sure, there is still a chance; perhaps you will hear from her when her self-confidence needs a boost or when she needs a favor. He may call you when he is in between flames or when he needs a

She shall pursue her lovers,
   But shall not find them.
Then she shall say,
"I will go and return to my first husband,
for it was better with me then than now."

HOSEA 2:7

sexual fix. "Oh yeah," he'll muse to himself as he thumbs through old names and telephone numbers, "this one worshiped the ground that I walked on!" Maybe she will take you back—then hurt you again. Only World War I and Ali's retirements were final.

Love Is Blind

Several of Rod Serling's *The Twilight Zone* episodes address the stark reality that our memory of the past is usually in vast contradiction to our recollection. People, places and events are not always as wonderful as we remember.

Time distorts memory, especially if we choose to deny and repress any unwanted realities (Memory). Through *selective memory*, you may have chosen to acknowledge and store that "wonderful" day in the park, choosing to overlook the argument that she provoked or the subtle comment that he made about the two of you not having enough in common. If you loved him, then naturally you were going to dismiss any unpleasant words or actions that may have transpired that day. As children, we try to avoid learning anything complex or take in anything uncomfortable. In author Anne Tyler's *The Accidental Tourist*, Macon Leary, a writer, is divorced by his wife Sarah. Macon, while longing for his wife to return, gets involved with another divorcee, Muriel Pritchett. To his delight and joyfulness, Sarah eventually returns to Macon, willing to give their relationship another chance, to which he of course promptly agrees. It is not long, however, before Sarah begins to criticize and berate Macon, continuing a behavior pattern that had existed during their marriage. Macon, having evolved since he had last been with his wife, realizes how stressful life had always been living with her, how critical that she had always been and is no longer willing to accept it. Ironically, he chooses to leave Sarah and returns to Muriel, whom he realizes had truly cared, nurtured and loved him for who he was.

Selective recall creates a glorified picture of your former lover and the relationship that you thought you had (Memory; World Book, Inc.). By reprogramming your memories, however, and by intentionally reassociating every trigger and refiltering every reminder with an undesirable one, you can begin to dispel much of the erroneous perception that you have stored away. Talk to your therapist. Talk to your friends, family and anyone else who had the occasion to meet her or him. It is difficult to get a bird's-eye view or to see the forest from the trees when you are in the middle of the wood. This perverted perception is erroneous as you will ultimately discover. Thus, objective observations from friends, professionals and other outside parties are enormously beneficial. *Charm is deceitful* (Pr. 31:30), and we think that we have lost the greatest thing on Earth. Other people will see things to which you have been blind and offer new insights and perspectives. Your "soul mate's" act, abuse, deceit and insanity may be oblivious to you right now but may be blatantly obvious to others. In time, it will be obvious to you, too.

Your former partner, for all that she or he has put you through recently, does not warrant occupying the invaluable space in your head or the tender chambers of your heart. As you continue to make retrospective observations about him or her, you'll gradually will them out of your memory through *motivated forgetting*. You will be able to do this by deliberately dismissing any positive memories and thinking about other interests, business and people in your life, likened to children who repeatedly lose and leave behind even their most precious possessions the moment something new, better or exciting deters their attention. S*elective memory reprogramming* and *motivated forgetting* will also be explored in later chapters.

Mr. & Ms. Rong

A relationship can either make you or break you. This one has broken you for the moment. You met the wrong person, and he hurt you, misled you, strung and failed to nurture you. He turned down a good opportunity with a good person, someone who loved, who cared, and you want this person back?

Einstein said that insanity was doing the same thing over and over again and expecting a different result. Short of talking it out with her or him and being willing to do your part in salvaging the relationship, there is nothing that you could have done to change this person or where fate led you. They would only have continued to extend their behavior pattern. Do not allow yourself to be victimized a second or third time. Do not entrust your happiness in the hands of someone else; rather, restore your identity, dignity, integrity and autonomy, and meet someone who wants to be with you. Do not set yourself up for more misery; you do not deserve to be mistreated or unloved, but you should want a loyal, loving and faithful partner who has your happiness at heart.

Judy is always home to greet her husband when he returns home from a long, hard day at work. She gives him a big warm hug and kiss, and within minutes the two of them sit down to a home-cooked dinner.

Julie breaks her back for hours, preparing dinner for her husband every night. It is truly a labor of love.

Amy wakes up extra early in the morning to prepare lunch for her husband who is always rushing out the door. The sandwiches are made with ham, lettuce, tomato, mayo and love.

Hsiaochen is always looking out for my welfare, concerned with my health and well-being and insisting that I bundle up when it is cold outside, suggesting that I eat right and preparing meals rich in nutrients.

Lydia was first on line at the pharmacy whenever her boyfriend caught ill. She made time to see him when he was sick and helped nurture him back to health.

Tom goes out of his way for his fiancée, showering her with gifts and much affection.

The Power of Positive Thinking

Which of you by being anxious can add to his stature a single cubit? (Mt. 7:27) An optimist is one who appreciates the glass being half full while a pessimist laments over it being half empty. The importance of positive thinking and the serious effects of negative thinking were addressed earlier. Spirituality plays a vital role in our mental outlook, and whether or not one wants to ascribe to the beneficial role that religion plays in one's life, he cannot deny the powerful effects of faith on religious or spiritual individuals. The devout rest in the knowledge and trust that a higher power exists; thus, many of them are genuinely happier people because of it. Religion has transformed the lives of countless numbers of people, saving them from the throes of depression and the brink of suicide. Dr. Norman Vincent Peal's *The Power of Positive Thinking* emphasized the immense psychological benefits of the belief in the power of God. Saint Paul encouraged us to be of good cheer and rest in the faith in God (Acts 27:24).

Profile of Mr. & Ms. Wright

He is sensible and not foolish, making logical decisions and acting on them without rashness and haste. She is reasonable and not devoid of common sense, avoiding ridiculous and ludicrous acts and speech. She is rational, wise and without absurdity. They choose their arguments wisely and do not break a special bond over a petty disagreement.

He is capable, ambitious and hard-working. She is not lame, lazy or dependent on her husband. He is not a parasite to his wife or anybody else.

She is not spoiled but one who can appreciate luxury, beauty and fine taste. She knows the value of fine and precious articles.

They should want to make an effort to please your family and friends and not shy away or avoid them as if they were *The Munsters* or *The Addams Family*.

I cannot think well of a man who sports with any woman's feelings; and there may often be a great deal more suffered than a stander-by can judge of.

Jane Austen

She is a genuine woman, capable of feelings and willing to experience the full range of emotions, and not possess a hardened heart or live in a fantasy world of bliss and unreality. She feels and expresses pain and sorrow as well as joy.

He is amenable to self-discovery, self-awareness and growth and does not consider himself perfect or above you and others.

He is easygoing and free from pettiness, not quarrelsome and always finding something to complain and fight about. She remembers to acknowledge his attributes and his virtues as well.

She has nice things to say about others and knows when to hold her tongue while in the company of friends and relatives.

He has strong family values and does not speak ill of his parents (*Holy Bible* 588-89; *New Translation of the Holy Scriptures* 866).

She respects God.

He is generous and not stingy. He wants the best for you that he can offer.

There is no seething inner core of resentment or contempt masked by a false layer of flattery or deceit. *The wounds inflicted by a lover are faithful, but the kisses of a hater are things to be entreated* (Proverbs).

He is not jealous; he trusts you.

He does not flee at the first sign of trouble but has the backbone to confront each conflict and battle as it arises.

"Relax, things are going to go wrong!" ensured the pastor to the newly wedded couple. He or she knows that discord is a normal and natural part of any relationship or marriage.

She can admit fault and not pass the blame with inane rationalization and excuses. He does not ostracize, judge or condemn; berate or mock you. Love and judgment do not coexist.

They are open-minded and tolerant of others. They are sincere and always tell the truth (*Holy Bible* 588-89; *New Translation of the Holy Scriptures* 866). Be leery of a man or woman who displays or exemplifies any of the following:

Warning Signs

- devoid of compassion
- devoid of emotion
- manipulative
- narcissistic
- cruel
- stingy
- unappreciative
- unpredictable
- two-faced
- irrational

Portrait of a Co Dependent

I compromise my own values and integrity to avoid your rejection or anger. I am very sensitive to how you are feeling and feel the same. I am extremely loyal, remaining in harmful situations too long. I am often afraid to express differing opinions and feelings of my own. I value your opinion and way of doing things more than my own. I put my values aside in order to connect with you. My good feelings about who I am stem from being liked by you. My fear of your anger determines what I say and do. The dreams I have for my future are linked to you. I do not perceive myself as a lovable or worthwhile human being (Being in a Codependent Relationship).

What *Might* Have Been

Co Dependence: Two Minus One Equals Zero

Relationships are not the answer to happiness. Indeed, they can mean your unhappiness and undoing. Perhaps this was a rebound romance following a previous broken relationship. A partner should not be someone who completes you but someone with whom you can share your completeness. Liking yourself comes first, and unless you possess a strong sense of identity, integrity and self-esteem and are in a healthy, mutually loving, caring and nurturing relationship with the right person, getting involved in an abusive and co dependent relationship with the wrong person can be catastrophic. Liken it to a bird who is free to fly anywhere within the boundaries of her cage. You may feel happy and have a false sense of security, but you pay with your identity, self-esteem, independence and growth (Being in a Codependent Relationship; The Patterns of Codependency), and like the puppy whose happiness and purpose in life lie in the hands of his master who no longer wants him, abandonment by the other can be devastating. You neither want your self-esteem and self-confidence to be at the mercy of someone else, nor do you want to continue to tiptoe, worrying about offending him or pleasing her.

A Marriage Made in Hell

You might have ended up unhappily married or divorced, at best, or the relationship would have lingered on indefinitely, leaving you even more devastated later on down the road. All relationships have a honeymoon phase, and we usually put our best foot forward initially. You would have seen their true colors eventually. An abusive relationship with the wrong person would have cost you your identity and self-integrity ultimately. Abusive partners especially, know how to exploit and capitalize on the weaknesses of their co dependent victims, using criticism, blame and guilt to control them, attributing to them their own problems, casting even more shame upon them and threatening to leave them lonely, helpless, needy and desperate. Or they will pull a sudden Dr. Jekyll and Mr. Hyde and abandon their partners without reason or provocation, absolving themselves of guilt and blame by attributing their reasons for the abandonment to a fault within the other, or equally disconcerting, without any explanation whatsoever. More often than not, people do know right from wrong. They do have the ability to control their actions and respect the dignity of others; however, for either a lack of control, regard for others and apathy, they choose to do injury. Many characteristics of abusive personalities exemplify those of sociopaths, psychopaths and people with schizoid and other antisocial personality disorders (Sylvia). From my own experience working with a considerable number of troubled youths over the years, it is clear that they are in fact aware of the immorality of their disrespectful, sometimes violent actions toward peers as well as authority figures. These are children who are repeatedly reprimanded, suspended, written up and forced to meet with the teacher, principal and their own parents or otherwise penalized for their actions. They are indeed aware that what they are doing is wrong, but more often than not it is of very little concern to them, not about the harm that they bring to others or the consequences to themselves. There is a fine

An Eagle sat high in the branches of a great Oak. "I want to get married," said the Eagle, "and I can't find a mate who can provide for me as I should like." "Take me," said the Kite. "I am so strong I can carry away an Ostrich in my talons as if it were a feather." The Eagle accepted the Kite immediately. But after the wedding, when the Kite flew away to find something to eat for his bride, all he had when he returned was a tiny Mouse. "Is that the Ostrich you talked about?" said the Eagle in disgust. "To win you, I would have promised you anything."

An Aesop Fable

line between cruelty and insanity, and whether you can determine abuse or mental illness at this time, chalk this experience up to bad luck, and be thankful that neither is present in your life any longer.

So Why Can't I Let Go?

"I'd never join a club that would allow a person like me to become a member," Woody Allen once said. We have determined the type(s) of partner(s) whom you have drawn into your life, seen that they exemplified the abuse, disrespect and deceit that have enveloped your life for so long and realized that you were ultimately better off without them. Yet you still miss them and wish that they would return. Perhaps you are glorifying even the most wretched person because you have not had the good fortune of meeting the right people, and you are not allowing the right people into your life because you are still trapped in a perpetuating need to repeat unhealthy choice patterns. You will hold more of an appreciation for the appropriate man or woman when s/he enters your life. You cannot recognize bad unless there was good with which to contrast it.

Imagine what your ideal partner would be like, or reflect on the positive and appealing traits of friends and partners who really did care and whom you did appreciate. There really are many nice people out there. God, time and destiny will bring one of them into your life when you least expect it. Pushing the process draws the wrong people into your life, setting you up for more hurt. If you are meant to be together with someone, then you shall be, and if not, then not even money, an elegant wardrobe or a private jet will win somebody over. Be patient.

Respite-respite and nepenthe, from thy
 memory of Lenore!
Quaff, oh quaff this kind nepenthe and
 forget this lost Lenore.

From The Raven by Edgar Allan Poe

Flying Solo

A hiatus from entering into a new relationship may be advisable right now. Rebound relationships are almost always doomed to failure. You have probably been accustomed to meeting the same (wrong) types of people. You may be extremely vulnerable at the moment, prone to repeating unhealthy patterns, and unless you take a step back and get a bird's-eye view of the kinds of mates that you have drawn into your life, then you stand a very good chance of meeting another person who will treat you the same as the other(s). Instead, start thinking about the ideal man or woman, and do not settle for anything less. When you are ready to shop for a new partner, shop in the right stores, and choose your merchandise very carefully. Reinforce thoughts of Mr. or Ms. Wright, and in time the universe may grant you your wish, and if not, then it is better to be alone than unhappily married or in an unhealthy, unhappy, destructive and demoralizing relationship.

Good Riddance

"If it looks like a duck, walks like a duck and quacks like a duck, then in all likelihood it is probably a duck," said Groucho Marx. Cease this compulsive and destructive adulation of your former partner. Put an end to this erroneous, rose-colored, idealistic perception of the one who let you get away. In time, when you look back on this person with a different, clearer, more unattached frame of mind, then you will be able to see what you do not see at the present moment. You will not be willing or able to tolerate what you put up with before, and you shall indeed be grateful for what did not happen. They might have made your life a living nightmare. Put an end to the idolatry. Stop romancing and start seeing reality. A common and useful tool that is used in behavior management is the *Pros and Cons List* (Linehan 169). You might have utilized this in the past for making big decisions. To reiterate, first make a list of all of the good things about having had this person in your life (Pros), then make a second list of all of the bad things about having had this person in your life (Cons). This column should include all of the miseries, disappointments and misfortunes that he or she brought you even before the parting as well as those that would most likely have arisen at some point in the future. In the Pros column, be sure to include all of the blessings that have come about as a result of the breakup. Look the columns over. Do the pros outweigh the cons?

Look at it from this perspective. Like a miserable job, a bad move, a loss or your worst nightmare, it is something that you should feel relieved and grateful for having escaped. *The Proverbs* warns that *their footsteps lead to the shades* (*The Holy Bible: New American Catholic Edition* 608). You need never want to see this person again. She is going to be someone else's problem now, and what she did to you, she will do to the next. In the meantime, there are many nice people out there waiting for you to recover.

Chapter Summary

You were in love with an image that you projected. In *Star Wars: The Empire Strikes Back*, an apprehensive Luke Skywalker asks the eminent Jedi Master Yoda what lies inside the cave that he is about to enter. Yoda cryptically replies, "Only what you take with you." He or she was not the deity whom you have made them out to be.

Wanting is always greater than having, and all too often we set ourselves up for great disappointments when we insist on acquiring that which we yearn for. Instead of projecting what might have *been*, try imagining what *might* have been. If you dream of him or her returning to you, then remember that nightmares can also be dreams. You are finally free of this unlucky, haphazard encounter, and in time you will perhaps be ready to meet your real dream mate if and when you choose to do so. You will know them when you see them, and they will know you. He will be your friend as well as your lover. She will look forward to seeing you, and you will look forward to seeing her. They will not hurt you. He or she will in fact be a true partner and stand by your side in the good times as well as the challenging ones. You need to place more trust in the universe. Trust God. He knows what is best for you at this time. He is not punishing you but teaching you a lesson and providing the tools that you need to grow. You do not question the sunshine or the storms that He brings forth, so why question what He is doing for you right now? You lived with insecurity and uncertainty long enough. You lacked self-esteem and would have abdicated your identity to please her eventually. You were allowed no voice of your own, and in fact your very opinions were used as weaponry against you when your X decided that he was through with you. You were willing to endure mind manipulations, constantly concerned with living up to the other's expectations and perpetually wondering what you did wrong.

You were criticized, judged and routinely treated without the respect that you deserved. You allowed this because you blindly believed those insulting and offensive remarks and attacks on your character, and since you felt lucky to have such a "wonderful" person in your life who actually "loved" you, you did not want to do anything to risk losing them even if it meant defending your own honor or perhaps your own family and friends. Because your personal expression was stifled, you lived in a perpetual state of anger

SHE DOES HIM GOOD AND NOT HARM,

ALL THE DAYS OF HER LIFE.

PROVERBS 31:12

toward others when the anger should have been directed at your partner. Your anger is being misdirected at yourself even now as you absolve him or her of any accountability for hurting you. Love is blind. It blinds us to the truth. Denial renders us even blinder. If you were to recall every red flag, every clue that this person was wrong from the start, then you would realize that this ship that passed in the night was fated to sink from the very moment that it set sail, similar to movies such as *The Poseidon Adventure*, whereby you know from the onset that disaster is looming, but much as the protective mother who is in denial of her child's misconduct in school, despite the testimonies of nine out of ten faculty members, we do not want to face a reality that was staring at us squarely in the face from even the first telephone conversation that this person was not right for us. Try to detach yourself from him or her. Imagine a friend of yours describing his or her partner's behaving toward them with the identical behavior that yours did toward you.

In Gratis

Benjamin Franklin said that one good husband is worth two good wives, for both are scarce; thus, when you meet someone who is really deserving of your heart and your tears, then you shall appreciate and value her or him that much more. In the meantime, be contented. Be thankful and have no anxiety. *When goods increase, they are increased that eat them* (Ec. 5:11). Be joyful. Breathe a sigh of relief as you say, "Thank God!" Thank the Heavens that someone hurtful is out of your life and that you are on the mend. Thank the Lord for the people in your life. Be thankful for your family and friends. Be appreciative in all circumstances, for all which blesses and befalls us is the will of the All Mighty. Acknowledge all that you have, all that you have had, all that you will have and all that you have seen, accomplished, overcome and enjoyed.

Above all, heed David's commandment to pay homage unceasingly to the All Mighty for all of His good works, for His enduring love, for all of the gifts that He provides and all that He has promised us (*The Holy Bible* 733). When we were children, my sisters and I used to pray on our knees each night, thanking God for all that we had and asking Him to provide these blessings to all who were not as fortunate. Even Freud and most therapists would agree that an attitude of gratitude is a healthy thing. The Pilgrims offered an entire Thanksgiving feast, giving thanks for being alive, having food to eat and shelter with which to house themselves. Be ever grateful in prayer and reflection for the food that you eat, the air that you breathe and the water that you drink.

THE HEART OF HER HUSBAND TRUSTS IN HER,

AND HE WILL HAVE NO LACK OF GAIN.

PROVERBS 31:11

Hsing Hsing Tsing
and
Her Long Lost King

Once upon a time, in a far off kingdom, there lived a beautiful princess named Hsing Hsing Tsing and her beloved king. Now the King was a mean and selfish tyrant who was not very well-liked or trusted among his subjects. He made many promises without any intention of ever keeping his word. And why should he? He was the ruler of all the land. Now not only was the King a cruel and deceiving dictator toward his subjects, but he was also an oppressive and unfaithful husband as well. He even flogged his princess from time to time for his amusement. He was a vicious and hideous monarch who ruled out of fear, punishment and threats of punishment. But the Princess was blind. She did not see what the people in the kingdom saw and loved him just as he was.

One day, the King decided to leave the castle to sow his royal oats with the other subjects in the kingdom. He seized on the Princess's blindness and ran off into the kingdom without her knowing. At first, she failed to realize that her husband had gone away even though others in the palace had tried to warn her of his despotism and unfaithfulness. But then, two years later, a fairy godmother appeared to her and with a wave of her magic wand, bestowed upon the Princess the gift of sight. The Princess now realized for herself what a hideous beast the King really was, yet she still missed her Law of the Land and prayed for his long awaited return. "How foolish," thought the others in the palace, "even with her newly acquired gift of sight, she still hopes and waits for his return?"

The Princess, angered by their gossip, summoned the Fairy Godmother back to the castle and bid her cast all the tale-tellers out from the kingdom. The Fairy Godmother did as she was told and removed all of them from the kingdom.

Well Princess Tsing finally could no longer take the loneliness and yearning that was in her heart and summoned the Fairy Godmother. "Thou shalt wave thy magic wand once again," she ordered, "and return to me my Lord and Master." "That is something which should never again be," cautioned the Fairy Godmother. "As thy fairy godmother, I have sworn to protect thee," she continued, "and this is something I cannot do for thine own good." The Princess, however, still demanded the return of her king. "Very well," she replied, "I shall grant thee thy wish, but thou must never blame me for having warned ye." "Thou must also be reminded that thou will hast no more wishes should I grant thee what thou hast bid." But the Princess insisted that the Fairy Godmother grant her this request.

The Fairy Godmother once again waved her magic wand, and the King instantly returned. Princess Tsing was elated. Her king had come back. Well, very shortly thereafter, the Princess began to feel very stifled, resentful and threatened by the King. Once again she bellowed the Fairy Godmother. "I do not understand; why is my king now behaving with such deceit, such belligerence, such tyranny? Why has he changed?" To this the Fairy Godmother replied, "My jaded, aphasic princess, it is not the King who has changed; it is thee." "When granted thee sight," she retorted, did you thus realize for thyself the hideous, cruel and deceitful rogue he truly was?" "I bid you cast him away at once with thy magic wand, for continue to live in this castle with him I cannot." "Hast thou forgotten already," the Fairy Godmother responded, "thy third wish was thy last and cast him away I cannot." "It is thy fate that ye must live with thy king till death do ye part." And they lived unhappily ever after.

They came to console with him and comfort him. And they sat with him seven days and seven nights, and no one spoke a word to him, for they saw that his suffering was very great.

The Book of JOB 2:11-13

If you are in the audience tonight
and you've never contemplated suicide,
then you've never been in love.
If you've never contemplated murder,
then you've never been divorced.

Christopher Titus

CHAPTER IV
Reach Out:
You Are Not Alone

CHAPTER IV: Reach Out: You Are Not Alone

If all our misfortunes were laid in one common heap whence everyone must take an equal portion, most people would be contented to take their own and depart.

Socrates

Misery Loves Company

Bring me a mustard seed from every household that has not experienced a loss, bid the sage to the woman weeping over the loss of her child. The woman, of course, returned to the sage empty handed, discovering solace through sharing. Support groups such as Co Dependents Anonymous (CoDa) provide support, encouragement, compassion and understanding by empathetic and caring individuals who have also experienced love loss. Attendance at these circles also greatly reduces personal notions that your situation or emotional condition is unusual or extreme. Remember that many people are, have or will experience abandonment at some time in their lives, but it would also be a good idea to know your audience before you reach out for words of wisdom, comfort and advice. The right words from the right sources will provide comfort, and in conjunction with time, therapy and other resources, contribute toward your recovery. The wrong words from the wrong sources, however, even if well-intentioned, could prove detrimental, intensifying your heartache, depression and already butchered self-image.

Speaking from Inexperience

Never take the advice of someone who has not had your kind of trouble, suggested Sydney J. Harris. Unless a man or woman has truly experienced love and was unwillingly on the receiving end of a separation, then he or she cannot be fully empathetic, compassionate or understanding. If you are not an animal lover, for instance, then you may not understand the devastation that a lost pet can bring to its guardian. People lose mates by death, but rejection is an extremely powerful and missing component. A recipient of a breakup deals not only with the intense pain of the loss itself but also with the languishing pain of rejection by someone whom they still love. This is not to say that a person who has lost his or her partner to death will not share much of the same pain that you are going through, but do not be surprised if he or she naively minimizes your ordeal in comparison. A divorcee is an excellent ear provided that he or she has been abandoned, again, unwillingly. There are many people on the receiving end of divorces or separations who may have already grown discontent or apart from their spouses as well, and the latter may have spared them the initiation, and this too can be devastating. A spouse who has only initiated the divorce may not completely understand the degree of your pain. Avoid talking to people who are still married to their first childhood sweethearts. Heartbreak is akin to and often accompanied by depression; thus, people who have experienced episodes of depression will be empathetic toward much of the emotional and physical insanity that you are feeling, but again, unless they have been in your shoes, they may not understand why. Reach out. Talk to people. Share your story and your pain. *This communicating of a man's self to a friend,* observed Sir Francis Bacon, *works two contrary effects for it redoubleth joy, and cutteth griefs in half.* This is not the time for independence and pride. The strong and silent suffer. It may pleasantly surprise you to learn that far more people are sensitive, compassionate, understanding and willing to help than those who are not. Keep the numbers and names of your friends and therapist on you at all times, in your pocket, your car and near your bed. Do not feel uncomfortable about calling them in your time of need. One day you shall return the favor. Also, remember to visit chat rooms and websites that are filled with separation and divorce stories similar to your own and worse.

To Whom It May Concern:

Even those with the best intentions may inadvertently dispense injurious words, attitudes and judgments, especially when speaking from experience that they do not have. Be loving, patient, supportive and encouraging. Avoid being judgmental or critical. Never pressure someone into putting it behind them and moving on. It will only intensify their depression. Let them know that they are not alone. Some people are more sensitive than others. S/he needs to know that the hurt will run its course at his or her own pace and that this pace is different for everyone. He needs to be reminded of all of the people in his life who do care and who have cared. Let him know that there are more people in his life who do love him. Name the names of friends, family and other relatives. Let her know that many people are thinking about her at this very moment. Assure him that what happened need not be taken personally. Assuage the guilt that they may be unnecessarily carrying around with them. Focus on their positive, unique points, their talents, abilities, gifts and accomplishments. Compliment them. Their self-esteem is probably suffering right now. This is not the time to be negative. You may make positive suggestions, but do not hold them accountable for following them. Above all, listen. The most important thing that we offer one another is a listening ear. A loving silence often has far more power to heal and to connect than the most well-intentioned words.

The following is a list of do's and do nots when dealing with or offering assistance to a heartbroken individual. For the forlorn, it will provide a reference of productive words of wisdom and comfort that you may hear from those concerned as well as naive and elemental comments from others that you might choose to reject:

There is a friend who sticks closer than a brother.
Proverbs 18:24

DO NOT   Say, "You're going to lose your friends." *Misfortune is the test of true friendship* (Aesop).

DO   Be a friend.

DO NOT   Abandon or avoid her.

DO   Continue to be an available resource. Be as available as you can for as long as you can. At the very least, let her know that you care. *In prosperity our friends know us; in adversity we know our friends* (John Churton Collins).

DO NOT   Ask, "Is there anything I can do?" (It is doubtful that they will hand you their grocery list.)

DO   Take the initiative. Do something beneficial for him. Cook a meal. Order something in. Buy something that you think would make her feel good. Provide inspirational literature. A book of crossword puzzles makes for hours of distraction and entertainment.

DO NOT   Say, "Go ahead, kill yourself!" (Self-explanatory)

DO   Take talk of self-harm seriously, but unless your friend is determined to hurt herself, do not panic or take the liberty of calling the police. Respect her dignity. You may ask her if she thinks that she needs to be admitted to an emergency room, but do not suggest it. A loving, supportive ear is often enough to avert a suicide attempt.

DO NOT   Berate the person.

DO   Acknowledge the person's attributes. (President Monroe once said that a little flattery will support one through difficult times.)

She weeps bitterly in the night, tears on her cheeks.
THE LAMENTATIONS OF JEREMIAH 1:2

DO NOT Say, "You're too sensitive." (Maybe you are not sensitive enough?)

DO Acknowledge their sensitivity as a special quality and an asset.

DO NOT Make comments suggesting mental illness (depression is a natural response to abandonment, akin to symptoms of trauma).

DO Let them know that what they are experiencing is normal, that they are not losing their mind and that the symptoms will not last forever.

DO NOT Say, "It was your fault!" (You might as well save them the trouble and pull the trigger yourself.)

DO Reinforce the loving and thoughtful things that he/she did for the other.

DO Reinforce the undesirable words, attitudes and actions of the other.

DO NOT Say, "It's your *choice* to be depressed." A broken heart, like a broken arm, takes time to mend. Letting go is a process, not a choice.

DO Say, "It gets better." (It does.)

DO NOT Say, "You're doing this for attention." Do not project your own motives onto someone else. It is true that there are chronic doomsayers, attention seekers, manipulators and compulsive liars, but do not underestimate another's bereavement and potential for self-harm, especially if this is not typical of her.

DO Say, "You have people who love and care about you." This is the time for compassion.

It's the friends you can call up at four a.m. that matter.

Marlene Dietrich (1901 - 1992)

He did not await anything with impatience and gave neither praise nor blame–he only listened.
Siddhartha

DO NOT Say, "Be strong!" (Actually it is those who are the strongest who can acknowledge and feel their pain to the fullest.)

DO Allow for and be tolerant of the person's pain, regardless of its duration and intensity. If you are truly a friend, then you will bear with them through this difficult time.

DO NOT Say, "Well if I were you then I'd..." (You are not them.)
DO NOT Judge.
DO Listen. Acknowledge. Understand. Validate. Repeat. Support.

DO NOT Say, "You should be over this by now," or "You have grieved long enough." *Never discourage anybody who continually makes progress, no matter how slow* (Plato). To expect one to "Get over it already" or "Move on" shows a lack of understanding and a lack of patience. It is also detrimental to their self-esteem. People are often powerless over their depression. If they could "snap out of it," they would. There is no rule. The time for recovery depends on the individual and the circumstances of the breakup.

DO Acknowledge that this is a very difficult time for them but that they will get through it at their own pace.

DO Share similar stories and cases. Let him know that he is not alone.

DO NOT Be the bearer of *good* news.
DO Maintain a similar, solemn countenance as the person you are trying to help (misery loves company, not good news).

DO NOT Say, "Smile!" It may mask her feelings from others, but repression of emotions will only prolong the depression. The only way out is through.

DO NOT Do anything that will pressure her to smile or laugh.

DO Highlight/help him acknowledge the positive.

DO NOT Encourage her to hide her feelings from the world. Acknowledging and sharing one's feelings are vital to healing.

DO Be open and approachable.

DO NOT Say, "It's such a great day! You should be out in the sun."

DO Remain in a place where s/he is most comfortable and feeling least insecure. In many cases, comfort can mean a dark room with a blanket. *Singing cheerful songs to a person whose heart is heavy is as bad as stealing someone's jacket in cold weather or rubbing salt in a wound* (Pr. 25:20).

DO NOT Say, "Only the weak get depressed." Depression is not a character flaw, and everybody is prone to it. One of our country's greatest presidents, Abraham Lincoln, suffered from depression most of his adult life.

DO Educate yourself on the subject.

DO NOT Make discouraging comments suggesting little or no progress.

DO Highlight any progress that has been made.

DO NOT Say, "Look how you've wasted your precious life!"

DO Say, "Positive changes and experiences arise from sadness." Remind them that some of the greatest works by writers and poets have been inspired during times of sorrow. Sorrow also increases one's capacity for compassion.

DO NOT Make references to karma or punishment.

DO Treat this as you would a death; for the abandoned it might as well be.

DO NOT Pressure the person to live up to erroneous and antiquated values and norms (e.g., "Men don't cry") or also to a man, "You're taking this like a 'woman.'"

DO Be complimentary; pay sincere compliments.

DO NOT Condemn the person for being too emotional.

DO NOT Expect that his emotions be controlled, rational and logical.

DO NOT Say, "Stop feeling sorry for yourself" or other synonymous words of wisdom such as "Get off the pity pot." The "kick-in-the-pants" method is not beneficial to everyone. Know your audience.

DO Show compassion.

DO Try to empathize and share the grief.

DO NOT Make random trite and ludicrous suggestions such as aroma candle therapy or a proper diet. (Swallowing a mouthful of vitamin supplements and lighting candles may please GNC and Yankee Candle Co., but it will not do a thing for your friend's recovery.)

DO Suggest therapy, a talk with a trusted clergy, prescription medication and inspirational literature.

He was a man of sorrows,
and acquainted with grief.
Isaiah 53:3

The tears that you spill, the sorrowful,
are sweeter than the laughter of snobs
and the guffaws of scoffers.
            Kahlil Gibran

DO NOT   Say, "It's not like they died!" (It probably would be easier if they had. Death does not carry the sting of rejection or betrayal.)

DO   Acknowledge the person's pain and love for the other person.

DO NOT   Say, "It's not like you were married!" (A marriage certificate entitles one to a broken heart?)

DO   Treat the abandonment as any other trauma.

DO NOT   Say, "You're using this as an excuse not to move on with your life" (more profound words of ignorance).

DO   Encourage and motivate her to make life pleasant and exciting.

DO NOT   Try to "motivate" the grief stricken by telling him that the other has "moved on."

My heart is sick, withered like grass,
    and I have lost my appetite,
Because of my groaning,
    I am reduced to skin and bones.
I lie awake,
    lonely as a solitary bird on the roof.
            Psalms 102:4-7

DO NOT Say, "I think that you enjoy being depressed!" (A suicidal person may become homicidal—to you.)

DO Try to be understanding. Try to empathize.

DO NOT Say, "You have nothing to be depressed about."

DO Offer condolences even if you do not think that the person has the "right" to be depressed. Recall your losses and how it felt when others minimized and trivialized them.

Friendship is certainly the finest balm
for the pangs of disappointed love.

Jane Austen

Dear Nick,

I am so sorry about your engagement! That poor girl didn't know she was getting something special - her loss. She was a fool to let you go. You're a great guy and anyone would be very fortunate to have you in their life. You're kindhearted, caring, loving and willing to help anyone who needs it, and above all, you're trusting. She knew that about you and she took advantage of that until she was ready to move on.

But it is for the best. She would have ended up hurting you much more if you had married her. You have become a different person because of this. It has made you grow and do things that you normally wouldn't have done. Things happen for a reason. Life will be better someday. I will always be here to help or just listen. Love, Janie

Just because your problems are many, don't think the rest of us haven't any.
Anonymous

Join the Crowd

There is a tale about a group of discontented people, each of whom was suffering from his or her cross to bear. Each individual was bid to place her or his cross in a central pile and then to subsequently return to the pile and pick the smallest, lightest cross they could find. They promptly did as they were instructed, each person taking the least burdensome cross among the large stack, picking up, ironically, the one that they had thrown into the pile originally. You do not have to look much farther than your own backyard to see that what has happened to you is about as prevalent as the common cold. Consider Hollywood alone: Liz; Cage and Presley; Bronstein and Stone; Cruise and Kidman; Barrymore and Green. Clint Eastwood's wife did not make his day suing for divorce, and certainly Nicole Kidman did not think that Tom Cruise was top gun after their ten year marriage ended.

Ryan took Pat for everything that she could and then disappeared one day never to be seen or heard from again.

Fran left Erin quite unexpectedly, especially since the two of them were considered to be a match made in heaven.

I have cried all day! I have no tears left. I can't seem to move on with this. It's harder than when Michael left. I'm back to the self-pity thing again. I can't sleep, can't eat, can't think. Why can't he see what he does to me? I am so tired of crying. I truly hate the holidays. People on the phone say, "You're getting the flu, you sound awful." If they only knew. I find myself wanting him to feel the hurt I feel because of him. I wonder if I will ever get over this.

It took eight years for Dana to learn that Sal never had any intention of staying with her.

Noel's relationship with Jody got off to a heavy, hot, romantic and passionate start. They talked about marriage and a future together. She told him how much she loved and cared. She told him that she could never live without him. She begged him to surprise her with an engagement ring, and within six months he delivered. That was when she ended their relationship.

Mel took his breakup with Kris so badly that he turned to drugs. Danny's ex still telephones, weeping incessantly after all of these months. Mark followed the girl who left him for months.

Young Love

They were classmates in the local middle school and going steady. One day, Johnny confided in his teacher that he wanted to end his life. Mary had met somebody new.

Suicide is the third leading cause of death among those 15 to 25 years of age and the sixth leading cause among those 5 to 14 years of age. Five thousand out of five hundred thousand attempts are successful. A breakup with a boyfriend or girlfriend can leave a teenager feeling so lost and alone that it seems as if death is the only option. A broken romance can be extremely traumatic for adolescents who have unrealistic expectations, self-esteem issues or a history of depression, and words of self-harm by a child should always be taken seriously. Their pain is just as real, and they are just as traumatized as adults, and more, for most lack the knowledge and experience to understand that rejection is universal and not a direct, personal affront. A child's self-concept is usually abysmally low at this age.

> And they called it puppy love.
>   Oh I guess they'll never know
> how a young heart really feels.
>   Donny Osmond

Out of the Mouth of Babes

My heart was broken by a boy in my class.
I don't know what happened. I didn't even do anything.
He had been playing me all along.

Daniela

She told me she liked me, and then broke up with me the next day. I was crushed! My family was very worried. They didn't think I'd ever get over it.

Eric

My head was so messed up!
It felt as if I were in another world.

Justin

All in the Same Boat

They left us just when we thought that everything was great. They told us that they loved us one day and then left us the next. They suddenly stopped calling us. We have all been strung along, slept with within weeks of being abandoned, promised the world, convinced that all was well and then finally left and devastated. We have blamed ourselves for the separation and have carried an enormous and unfair burden of guilt for far too long. We thought that we would never get over it, but we have all overcome it with time and perseverance, and so shall you.

Why she had to go I don't know, she wouldn't say.
John Lennon & Paul McCartney

But the wound still smarted. Siddhartha thought yearningly and let the pain gnaw at him, underwent all the follies of love. One day, when the wound was smarting terribly, Siddhartha rowed across the river, consumed by longing, and got out of the boat with the purpose of going to the town to seek his son...

Chapter Summary

There is a Swedish proverb which states that shared sorrow is half a sorrow. Although it is a common generalization that men tend to suppress their emotions, thereby intensifying their pain, today, for men and women alike, reaching out to wise and experienced sources will profoundly mitigate emotional pain.

Get on the telephone. Call your friends and supportive others. E-mail your friends and confidants. Talk to others who have been there. Join a support group. Read other inspirational and self-help literature on the subject. Join chat rooms on the Internet, and search the Web for breakup and divorce sites, and read the hundreds of posted stories that are similar, if not more devastating than yours.

Be discriminate in choosing your audience when reaching out to others. Console with experienced, understanding, sensitive and empathetic people, and take with a grain of salt those comments and words of advice given by others. Remember that nine out of ten people will be sympathetic and willing to help you. Filter out that ten percent who are not supportive or understanding of the difficulties that you are enduring.

You do not have to suffer in silence. You are not alone. As with losing loved ones through death, broken relationships are part of life and we all experience it ultimately.

...The wound still smarted; he still rebelled against his fate. There was still no serenity and conquest of his suffering. As he went on speaking and Vasudeva listened, he felt his troubles, his anxieties and his secret hopes flow across to him and then return again. Disclosing his wound to this listener was the same as bathing it in the river, until it became cool and one with the river. Siddhartha listened {to the river}. All of the yearnings, all of the sorrows, all the pleasures, all the good and evil, all of them together was the world. From that hour Siddhartha ceased to fight against his destiny. His wound was healing, his pain was dispersing.

Siddhartha

MALICIOUS WITNESSES TESTIFY AGAINST ME.

THEY ACCUSE ME OF THINGS I DON'T EVEN KNOW ABOUT.

THEY REPAY ME WITH EVIL FOR THE GOOD I DO.

I AM SICK WITH DESPAIR.

YET WHEN THEY WERE ILL,

I GRIEVED FOR THEM.

I WAS SAD, AS THOUGH THEY WERE MY FRIENDS OR FAMILY

AS IF I WERE GRIEVING FOR MY OWN MOTHER.

PSALMS 35:11-14

The Prayer of St Francis

Lord, make me an instrument of your peace.

Where there is hatred . . . let me sow love

Where there is injury . . . pardon

Where there is doubt . . . faith

Where there is despair . . . hope

Where there is darkness . . . light

Where there is sadness . . . joy

Divine Master,

grant that i may not so much seek

To be consoled . . . as to console

To be understood . . . as to understand,

To be loved . . . as to love

For it is in giving . . . that we receive,

It is in pardoning, that we are pardoned,

It is in dying . . . that we are born to eternal life

CHAPTER V
Forgive-And Forget

CHAPTER V: Forgive-And Forget

A God's Eye View
In God's Hands–And out of Yours

A man's mind plans his way, but the Lord directs his steps (Pr 16:9). There are things that come easily and naturally to us while at other times it seems that we never quite get what we want no matter how hard we try. Certainly you have aced a test that you were so certain that you had failed or have been rejected for a job even after you were confident that you had passed the interview with flying colors. Life seems to lead us by the nose many times, doesn't it?

If you have done everything humanly possible to save the relationship, then it is time to liberate yourself from this maddening guilt. There is simply nothing else you can do. The ball is in their court now. The Greek god Atlas, punished by Zeus for revolting, was doomed to carry the weight of the Earth upon his shoulders for eternity. You are not Atlas. You are not a beast of burden. Release the burden that you have self-imposed. Throw the ball back. She hurt *you*. Has *she* reached out? Does *she* feel remorse? Relationships are about two people. Marriage is an oath by the bride and groom to love and care for each other in sickness and in health; in sadness and sorrow; for better or for worse as long as they both shall live. It takes two to make this possible, both persons wanting to share this dream. The man or woman who chose not to walk this path with you obviously had other plans for him- or herself, and they were not the same as yours. They had a will, the free choice and the opportunity to stay with or return to you, and they chose not to do this. Thus, if you have done everything that you could to keep the relationship alive, apologizing and willing to make adjustments and amends, and they still want out, then it is out of your hands. You no longer have any say or control over this situation any more than you have a choice over tomorrow's weather.

Others will be cruel; we shall not be cruel. Thus, one should incline the mind.

Majjhima Nikaya

LET TING GO

R_X Forgive-And Forget

Forgive not seven times, bid Christ to Peter, *but seventy times seven.* "What?" "Forgive *him*?" "Shouldn't it be the other way around?" "But she hurt me!" "I'll never forget this for as long as I live!" You are most likely feeling self-pity right now, and while this is indeed quite understandable considering the circumstances, it is also very destructive and signifies a perpetual "Woe-is-me!" attitude or an "I'm not OK you are OK" perspective. This perception is extremely disempowering for you and quite empowering for them. We were always told to be the better person, to forgive and forget. Forgiveness is more than just "the moral thing to do" but a necessary step toward freeing yourself from the bonds of depression (Henderson). You can release a significant portion of your depression and resentment through forgiveness, and you can acquire the capacity to forgive by depersonalizing what the person did, understanding that their actions said more about them than they did about you. Anger and depression are synonymous, and rage stems from personalizing or internalizing the actions of others. "They don't know any better," you have heard it said. All of us are products of our life experiences and our environment. What we deal out is what we were dealt and what we know. We can also acquire the capacity for forgiveness and tolerance for ourselves and others, especially our former mates, by understanding that nobody is born perfect. Everybody has his or her own issues, and no one is exempt. You are not the only one with psychological luggage. We find ourselves hurt and offended because, paradoxically, we are glorifying those by whom we are offended, at the expense of our own self-worth (FitzMaurice), harmfully perpetuating this false and unrealistic perception.

One thing you will probably remember well is anytime you forgive and forget.
Franklin P. Jones

In *The Parable of the Unforgiving Servant*, it is not merely suggested that we forgive those who have wronged us but ordered. We have been given an ultimatum not a choice. We are continually torn between God's mercy, however, and our human desire for retribution. This internal anger and resentment is harmful, if not deadly, for these feelings actually reverse direction and inflict us with equal measure (Felluga). We have all experienced this madness for ourselves, to some extent, and have also witnessed its devastating effects on others. An ancient Chinese adage tells us that anger burns only the angry and that those who seek revenge had better be prepared to dig two graves.

You can acquire the capacity to forgive someone who has harmed you emotionally or physically by being sensitive, understanding and compassionate enough to realize that how others treat the world is a reflection of how the world treated them. Thus, one who has been abandoned, misled, hurt or otherwise mistreated during his childhood rearing will likewise treat his or her partner accordingly. Be the better of the two of you, for *it is only the weak who can never forgive*, according to Mahatma Gandhi, and *forgiveness is the attribute of the strong*.

God has granted us permission to forgive ourselves and one another, and once we do that, our guilt-produced illnesses go away, as in the story of the paralytic from the *New Testament* (Rifkin). Home is where the heart is, and if Freud's theory of *repetition compulsion*, or *transference* is valid, and we are indeed subconsciously obsessed with the return of a malevolent partner with whom we wish to even the score for an abusive parent, teacher, molester or childhood ruffian, then resolution in the absence of the aforementioned figures can only be accomplished through forgiveness (Felluga).

Keep on releasing and you will be released.
Luke 6:37

In the aforesaid parable, the king has the unforgiving servant thrown into jail, imprisoned and cut off from life itself. Sigmund Freud tried to express the truth of this parable using the language of modern psychology. He compared our journey through life to a long march down an imaginary road.

"At birth," claimed Freud, "each of us is supplied with a certain number of soldiers that we may deploy when we come across some opponent, some threat to our safety or some enemy, real or imagined. When we have a conflict with a neighbor that we cannot resolve, when we hold close to our hearts some anger or resentment, then we must station some troops at that point along the road. We must tie up some energy there, and that of course leaves us with fewer resources and fewer troops in facing the next challenge that presents itself. That is the reason why some of us, having marshaled so many of our reserves to fight so many ancient battles, have so little energy left for the challenges that confront us in the present. At bottom, we are asked to forgive, not because any of us has such a great supply of charity that we can rise above our differences with our neighbors but rather because we must let go of our anger and resentment or we shall die" (Henderson). When we clutch our judgments and our accusations close to our hearts, our hearts themselves are poisoned. For our own sakes and for our very salvation, we need to pray that we find the grace to forgive in our neighbors what God has already forgiven in us. Give thanks to God for a mercy strong enough and bold enough to set us free from this captivity.

In reading the Gospels, one can sense the pervading message of forgiveness and humility as well as loving-kindness. Lines in the *New Testament* such as *Turn the other cheek* and *If anyone would sue you and take away your coat, let them have your cloak*, suggest an exceptional attitude of passivity, even consenting exploitation from others. It is akin to what Gandhi termed *passive resistance*. Alan Watts phrased it *The Law of Reversed Effort*, a mystifying paradox. This doctrine of submissiveness contradicts our traditional American notions of strength and honor while the stance of the former paradoxically liberates us from the burden induced by the same postures.

A Psychological Martial Art

Mom told you to ignore the bullies while dad insisted that you stoop to their primitive level and fight back. You watched your manager maintain his composure and dignity as he allowed the customers' remarks to roll off his back, serving as a model for you. You tried "The Customer Is Always Right" approach for yourself and were amazed at how foolish it made the irate patrons feel when they humbly begged, "Please forgive me for the way I spoke to you!" You have seen it stated in the *New Testament* to forgive and resist not evil while many prophets and philosophers from many religions preached similar acts of virtue.

The spiritual path is not the enhancement of self-improvement or self-esteem but the goal of becoming holy (Lozoff). Holy does not always mean bliss; although, if we adhere to spiritual tenets and truths, then we are naturally more likely to live more peaceful lives with a minimum of strife, struggle and disappointment. Even the most reverent among us gets offended, angry and hurt by the people around us, but we, in seeking the way of the spiritual, must try to respond in truth and God's law in whatever and whomever comes our way as we tread the precarious and often unpaved path of life. It may be challenging at times, dealing with difficult people and circumstances, but we improve with practice. As always, the most difficult yet inscrutably simplest step along this road is the first. If you want to live the spiritual life, then do what Christ, the Dalai Lama, Mother Teresa and all of the saints and prophets of the ages would do. Be nice to the clerk at the Department of Motor Vehicles, refrain from confronting the inconsiderate neighbor next door, show compassion for the driver who is always in a frantic rush to get nowhere, and forgive your former spouse and others who have hurt you.

In martial arts such as judo or tai chi, the student learns how to ward off his opponent's strength and force away from himself, instead of resisting or absorbing it, and avoid physical harm, while the latter is consequently deflected off balance with equal magnitude, meeting peril at the fate of his own hands, force, weight and speed.

His own power is used against him, and like a boomerang, he gets back what he hurls (Martial Arts). Our initial feeling or impulse toward someone who offends us is often one of seething hostility and resentment–to resist, hate back, hold a grudge or seek revenge (*an eye for an eye*). This is largely due to internalizing others' behavior toward us. Fight fire with fire and you get burned; walk away from it, and you save your skin and your life. *A prudent man sees danger and hides himself.* (Pr. 27:12) If you have ever once tried the inverse approach of responding to someone else's hostility with friendliness and benevolence, then you know the tremendous sense of relief that you feel. "Kill them with kindness," mom might have told you, "because it is hard to stay angry at someone who is not angry back." Retaliation may release anger and bitterness, but loving-kindness dissipates it, and unless the person is just plain heartless, then there is sure to be some guilt and remorse for his actions and behavior.

How often have you mustered up the courage to stand up to the childhood bully, your boss or the inconsiderate next door neighbor only to find yourself in reoccurring battles? Did you really earn their respect after that fighting and heartache, or did your actions incite repercussions that would come back to haunt you in some obvious or even subtle way? It is an exceptional person who will admit to having done wrong. Most people cannot accept the dastardly side of their nature and absolve themselves of their wrongdoing at others' expense instead of owning up to their behaviors even if they know they are at fault. World War I, the great triumph of good over evil and "war to end all wars," merely set the stage for World War II.

If a wise man has an argument with a fool, the fool only rages and laughs (Pr. 29:9). Take the path of least resistance, you have heard it advised. Research shows that confronting or resisting people who cause us distress does not solve the problem but may actually escalate it, especially if they inflict pain as a means of control and

> Look how he abused me and beat me,
> Live with such thoughts and you live in hate.
> From the Dhammapada

dominance over others. While ignoring is probably our strongest arsenal against these individuals, it is quite a different matter when it is the man or woman whom we love who treats us so hideously. However, whether it is the neighbor provoking you, your supervisor mistreating you, a coworker offending you or your lover hurting you, it is probably the wisest strategy at your disposal to avoid taking them personally, understand that it says something about *them*, walk away and triumph through personal accomplishment, success and happiness. You do not stand alone, and this is not necessarily about you, so ignore them, and avoid the compulsion to descend to that which is beneath your level and dignity. We are powerless to change the minds of the mindless or the hearts of the heartless. It is often a futile attempt for one to change the dispositions of other people. Likewise, it would most likely be a fruitless endeavor to change the nature of your former fiancé. Your vain attempts to do so will only result in frustration and more hurt. If you really want to get even with your former lover or anybody else who has hurt you in the past, then forgive them.

Truth or Consequences

Psychologists claim that depression is misdirected (inward) anger that we hold against others. Suicide, for example, is actually a repressed feeling of homicide, perhaps toward your ex or the world at large. Naturally we cannot unleash our rage on either, so we choose the target of least threat and resistance—ourselves. As children, we expressed our rage through temper tantrums, destroying our personal property and directing other acts of harm toward ourselves, because we were unable to draw these feelings toward our parents directly. As adults, we may even be given to banging our heads against or putting our fists through the wall, wounding ourselves in the process.

When we refuse to forgive, when we harbor resentment, we place our emotional and psychological well-being at risk (Henderson); therefore, for our own sakes as well as for our salvation, we have no other alternative but to pardon the person who has harmed us. When Christ preached forgiveness to his disciples, He was not only speaking from a moral standpoint but also as a counselor, advising them on how to live their lives with a happier and healthier attitude. The prophets and saints were those who were able to see the illusion of the physical world and all of our experiences within it as merely the background or the vehicles from where we grapple with and find our faith, learn and practice forgiveness, compassion and loving-kindness (Lozoff). The blind or faithless are those who reverse background and foreground, losing this spiritual perspective. Given the agonizing experience of another person causing you emotional distress, for example, you can exercise faith and God's will by being compassionate and forgiving yourself. This is easier said than done, naturally, but love, forgiveness, kindness, compassion and humility are the ways of the spiritual, versus the angry, resentful, vindictive, aggressive and arrogant ways of the blind and faithless. It is no wonder why we often hear people ask, "What faith do you *practice?*" Love, compassion and forgiveness are something that we practice from moment to moment; situation to situation and from trial to trial. These virtues and spiritual values are more than just the nice thing to do. They are God's laws.

Do not say, "I will do to him as he has done to me." (Pr. 24:29) We are not in a position to cast judgment, condemn or will punishment on anybody. That is up to God and God alone. Doing so will only perpetuate the anger and bitterness that you fester. *Rejoice not when your enemy falls and when he stumbles, let not your heart exult, lest the Lord see it, be displeased with you and withdraw his wrath from your enemy* (Pr. 24:17-18). Kindness works. Forgiveness heals. It frees you from the bondage of the oppressor whom you wish to serve (Henderson), and it allows you to be happy and healthy by

Look how he abused me and beat me,
Abandon such thoughts, and live in love.

From the Dhammapada

giving you back your right to be free (Lozoff). *Those who have not had your opportunities deserve your compassion*, said Richard Hittleman. *Sincere forgiveness isn't colored with expectations that the other person apologizes or change*, says Sara Paddison (Primal Page). *Don't worry whether or not they finally understand you. Love them and release them. Life feeds back truth to people in its own way and time.* Release the resentment toward the one who hurt you. Release the hostility. Be the better person. Forgive her. Forgive him. Forgive them all. *There but for the grace of God go I.* Do the math. Four hundred ninety *I forgive you's* should do the trick (Mt. 18:21). Similarly, if their return nourishes the mind's compulsion to reexperience trauma, then we as people who demand respect from ourselves and others should be motivated to put the experience behind us sooner rather than later.

Somebody once said that forgiveness is our giving up our right to hurt another for hurting us. Perhaps if you were able to get outside of yourself and inside of the one who has hurt you, then you might even waive that right willingly. A large proportion of our trouble derives from a subconscious tendency to compare ourselves to others, namely those whom we have lost, and our tendency is to come up short. If we could but look outside of ourselves, past our projections, judgments, assumptions, needs and self-deprecation, then we would see more clearly who it was that brought us despair. We would dispel the illusionary that we have cast for ourselves. You need not feel the need to do battle when you can deconsecrate your glorified other half and rise above him or her. The sting of a loss can penetrate deep within us, cracking the very core of our self-esteem, which has already been slow in decaying.

Nothing Personal

According to Freud, when we personalize or internalize the actions or words of another, we experience an affront to our ego, our false representation of our inner id to the world, resulting in struggling, guilt-crippling and even suicidal tendencies (Felluga). Eastern philosophy speaks of the *Self*, also termed the *soul* by many

Christian believers. We make a vain attempt to protect our inner core of insecurity and inadequacy with a phantom exterior, which only serves to repress those feelings against which the *super ego* feels compelled to protect us. Abrasive and unreasonable behavior directed at us from others emanates from a world of abuse and mistreatment. We really do not know from whence they came, what they saw and what they experienced, yet we internalize abuse, evil, sometimes insane behavior from others, somehow assuming that the defect lies within ourselves. This generates anger, resentment and a whole syndrome of destructive emotions, all of which can be mitigated considerably by taking the behavior from where it arises and doing so benevolently. Mental illness is a disease or disorder of the brain not unlike heart disease. We do not chastise victims of heart disease. Mental illness or depression is not something that you can just talk yourself out of or purge with a candy bar or ice cream cone. If that were the case, then Nestles and Haagen-Dazs would put an alarming number of psychiatrists out of work.

A Reflection from Without

"It's not you." "Look where it is coming from." "Consider the source." You have heard these words of consolation before and not necessarily to be meant as an attack on anybody but for a very good reason. Perhaps you are feeling sorry for the wrong person. Instead of self-indulging in your own misery, secretly offer condolences to him or her. *Make them the object of your pity* (1 K. 8:50). She might have been born unlucky. He might have been a bad seed. There are many people out there who are compelled to bring harm to others. Just turn on the news. Many know that what they are doing is immoral but cannot control their actions.

Hereditary illnesses or predispositions, schizophrenia and mood disorders run in families, and early life experiences such as the loss of a parent, child abuse and even accidents may affect an individual's ability to adapt to changes or to recover from painful events (Andreason). Numerous children exhibit the identical antisocial personality traits as their older and younger siblings and their parents. One might readily become impatient, even offended by these troubled youngsters; however, it takes just a little understanding and knowledge from without to be compassionate enough to realize that these children, and their parents alike, are truly scarred and not of their own free will. The scar consists of changed anatomy and chemistry within the brain, perhaps induced by injury during or after the prenatal phase and alcohol, nicotine or drug abuse by the parent during the fetal stage. Even severe maternal stress can imprint itself on the fetus. The mother might have been full of anger internally, hating the fetus, or resenting, fearing or feeling deeply disappointed and neglected by its father (Primal Page). According to Frank Lake in *Theology and Personality*, the pain of the world picked up by the family is funneled by the mother into the fetus. The fetus receives all of these messages. Existing grief, misery, pain and suffering as well as socioeconomic problems can all be attributing factors to the stress and negativity that a mother may bring to the unborn child. The birth experience itself is also a factor. *Birth, Death and Organic Energy* from *Primal Community* maintains that the pre-born does not have the words. It only has the biological patterns that eventually give rise to the words. When birth trauma is significant, every detail of impingement and reaction is etched on the memory.

As long as we are human beings with egos, it is going to require time and effort to cease internalizing their actions. What individuals with personality disorders need, however, are understanding and compassion as opposed to anger, impatience and insensitivity.

R̲x̲ The Mantra

A mantra is a chant, a mystical incantation that can take the form of a series of repetitious phrases such as affirmations used to reprogram the subconscious. The subconscious mind is a reflection of what we feed it. This mind-shaping device is not at all new to psychology. It is the basis of hypnotism and probably the most scientific explanation of prayer. The mantra is a common meditation technique used in a number of Eastern religions. It is retraining and reprogramming the mind, which has been programmed with negativity and misguided values. You can create one or more mantras by first highlighting the sentences or phrases contained herein that you have found to be most helpful. List them on a piece of paper, or write each on a separate post-it or index card, and then repeat them to yourself over and over and over again, much as you would a Rosary or test cram session. The right mantra will also provide some temporary relief from your depression. General one-line mantras might include "It's not about me," "I've done all I could," "I was very good to her/ him," "Make *them* the object of your pity," "Everything falls into place," "This too shall pass" and "I take responsibility for allowing someone such as this into my life."

Forgiveness is the key to action and freedom

Hannah Arendt

A Mantra for Forgiveness

I forgive you! I forgive you!

I forgive you! I forgive you!

I forgive you! I forgive you!

I forgive you! I forgive you!

I forgive you! I forgive you!

Anger makes you smaller, while forgiveness forces you to grow beyond what you were.

Cherie Carter-Scott

Time heals all wounds, it is said, but forgiveness can certainly expedite that time. Second only to our choice to ignore, forgiveness is probably our greatest defense against personal insult and injury (Mayer). Our inclination to internalize the words, actions and attitudes from those around us, however, almost always makes us forget that we have so powerful a weapon at our disposal, and it requires no physical or verbal action from us but merely a choice. Christ, the saints, prophets, sages and even Freud knew of the power of forgiveness (see also Miracosta and Frances). These were people who were able to step outside of their own egos and ego defenses and recognize that people are not flawless. Some people have better control over their shortcomings while others do not.

You may feel it too soon to forgive the one who hurt you at the moment, but in time you will find it not only easier but necessary.

Forgiveness is almost a selfish act because of its immense benefits to the one who forgives.

Lawana Blackwell

Practice forgiveness. Release every individual against whom you've harbored resentment.

- *your ex-wife who took everything from you*

- *an abusive parent*

- *your partner who embezzled*

- *your mother who passed away*

- *your father who abandoned you*

- *your friend who deserted you*

- *your friends and family who failed to support you when you needed them*

- *your supervisor who passed you up for promotion after your faithful years of service*

To err is human; to forgive infrequent.
Franklin P. Adams

Others with whom you can practice forgiveness:

- *your neighbor who annoyed you*

- *your daughter who deserted you*

- *your boss who demeaned you*

- *your employer who let you go*

- *the man who robbed you*

- *your sister who cheated you*

- *your lover who didn't love you*

- *your ex-husband who threatened you*

- *your children who don't appreciate you*

- *the mystery driver who banged up your fender*

- *a confidant who disappointed you*

Whether it concerns our parents, grandparents, nieces, nephews, old acquaintances, schoolmates or our previous lover, forgiveness is liberating, and as with anything else worthwhile, it takes time, practice and commitment, hence the reason for its required innumerous repetition. But the results are undoubtedly well worth the effort. Practice forgiving people other than your ex as well. *Being hated, don't give way to hating*, wrote Rudyard Kipling. It is certainly a happier and healthier option than practicing and perpetuating resentment and bitterness.

Forgetting

If anyone will not receive you, shake off the dust from your feet as you leave (Mt. 10:13-14). The woman who hurt Rob "does not mean a thing" to him anymore. According to Freud's concept of *interference*, it is the acquisition of new information and the motivated forgetting or conscious repression of threatening thoughts, memories and feelings that will interfere with the recall of previously stored information. Thus, through Homme's parallel concept *of avoidance learning*, painful memories can be avoided by thinking about something else (Mayer).

People forget more and more as time passes (Loftus). Through time and *motivated forgetting* (Felluga), we can gradually erase or diminish painful and glorified memories and images and replace them with realistic ones. Hence, if it is the mind's function to repress unpleasant memories in favor of the pleasant ones, which have the adverse effect of glorifying a person and relationship we had, then

"A well-taught noble disciple understands what things are fit for attention and what things are unfit for attention. Such a person does not dwell upon to those things unfit for attention."

Majjihma Nikaya

we would want to replace and inversely repress the pleasant memories in favor of the unpleasant ones, along with the factor of time, and reinforce the undesirable traits of our former mates and the difficult memories attached (Kornfield 71). As with anything else disconcerting, it should be your conscious will to forget a person and a memory that have brought you so much anguish.

Repetition

Liken memory to a muscle. The more you work it, the stronger it becomes. Conversely, through disuse, it weakens. This is the concept behind mantras and affirmations, a regular and continuous repetition of unexampled thoughts and attitudes. Our utopian memories and perception of our former partner and relationship, therefore, must be replaced and reinforced with realistic ones in their stead.

Associate–Dissociate–Preassociate–Reassociate

Any arising thought of your former match must promptly be associated with an undesirable one. If it is triggered by something familiar, a reminder for example, then you must try to break the association that stimulus had with the person and substitute it with that of another person or era in your life, per se, that came before or after s/he came into your life. Through repetition of substitutions and repression of thought, in addition to time, compulsive thoughts and memories will diminish. Their priorities changed, and yours shall, too.

> Pray for those who hurt
>   you.
> When things are taken away from
>   you, don't try to get them back.
> You must be compassionate.
>   Luke 6:28-36

Chapter Summary

Forgive...

A wise friend once said that the reason that he bore no malice toward those who had hurt him was because he felt that he had been blessed with a very fortunate life as opposed to those who sought his harm, an antithetically simple attitude of profundity and magnanimity.

Forgiveness is a product of compassion and depersonalization, which are the inverse of self-absorption and personalization; thus, the more we step back and take the time out to show compassion rather than personalize and get wrapped up in our own minds, the greater the quotient. We are often victims of circumstance and have no control over the behavior patterns of others. It is easier to forgive when we do not personalize.

Although I cannot forget, I am choosing to forgive. Nancy

I actually feel sorry for Robin!   This is all about him.
He'll just go on sabotaging his relationships.   Alex

...And Forget

Enjoy. Plan. Project. Accomplish. It shall be scary. Setting out to accomplish something for the first time is usually fraught with anxiety and uncertainty, but then it makes our lives something upon that is worth looking back. Everything happens for a reason.

Parable of the Unforgiving Servant

Therefore the kingdom of heaven may be compared to a king who wished to settle accounts with his servants. When he began the reckoning, one was brought to him who owed him ten thousand talents; and as he could not pay, his lord ordered him to be sold, with his wife and children and all that he had, and payment to be made. So the servant fell on his knees, imploring him, 'Lord, have patience with me, and I will pay you everything.' And out of pity for him the lord of that servant released him and forgave him the debt. But that same servant, as he went out, came upon one of his fellow servants who owed him a hundred denarii; and seizing him by the throat he said, 'Pay what you owe.' So his fellow servant fell down and besought him. 'Have patience with me, and I will pay you.' He refused and went and put him in prison till he should pay the debt. When his fellow servants saw what had taken place, they were greatly distressed, and they went and reported to their lord all that had taken place. Then his lord summoned him and said to him, 'You wicked servant! I forgave you all that debt because you besought me; and should not you have had mercy on your fellow servant, as I have had mercy on you?' And in anger his lord delivered him to the jailors, till he should pay all his debt. So also my heavenly Father will do to every one of you, if you do not forgive your brother from your heart.

Matthew 18:23-35

You know quite well, deep within you, that there is only a single magic, a single power, a single salvation…and that is called loving. Well, then, love your suffering. Do not resist it, do not flee from it. It is your aversion that hurts, nothing else.

Hermann Hesse

CHAPTER VI
Let Time Heal

CHAPTER VI: Let Time Heal

From the Depths of Despair...

Your heart feels as if it is going to burst right out of your chest. You feel like John Hurt in Ridley Scott's *Alien.* You almost wish that it would. You have lost more pounds in a week than the British stockholders did during *their* great depression. Now you actually want to *gain* weight. Even your underwear is sliding down.

You're traveling to another dimension. There's a signpost up ahead, your next stop, "The Twilight Zone." You feel as if you are in a world of balloons, clowns and distortions, similar to the fun house at the amusement park, only it is not fun, and you are not amused. Your TV is watching *you.* Mel Brooks's *High Anxiety* no longer makes you laugh.

You downed that Johnny Walker Blue Label Scotch that you had so frugally and selfishly sipped only twice in the past five years in five minutes. "Sir, don't you think you've had enough?" hints the bartender who is very concerned about his license and whether or not you will be able to pay your tab.

You have spent your whole life savings in a month. You have not taken a bath in a month either.

Mountain climbing, riding motorcycles, parachuting and flying helicopters–over Iraq–suddenly appeal to you.

The lyrics to Jim Morrison's "The End" make sense to you now. Romeo and Juliet were not so silly after all, and neither were all of those "pathetic," "foolish," "crazy," hopeless romantics toward whom you now wish you would have been more sympathetic and compassionate.

"I have not seen you since your First Holy Communion," Fr. Reilly recollects. Rabbi Gross claims that he has never seen you before.

You are obsessed with speeding bullets, powerful locomotives and leaping tall buildings in a single bound, but if you have considered attempting George Reeves's final stunt up in the sky, then you had better fly yourself right into the arms of a loving family member or friend or the office of a competent and caring psychiatrist or therapist. And if you are really serious about leaping before you look, then get yourself to the nearest ER before you finish reading this sentence.

It feels as if you were hit by a freight train. Your world is cold and dark. You cannot shut the tears off. You want to hide under the covers and die. You go hours and even days without eating or sleeping. You conceive outrageous plans to take your life and wait for the perfect opportunity to do so. You see him or her in just about everyone and everything that comes your way.

Let me assure you that you are not losing your mind. The descriptions in the aforementioned paragraphs are quite typical of depression. It is pure Hell while you are going through it, but the symptoms do dissipate. Your brain chemistry might have been knocked off balance, and you may even need prescribed medication for a while, but it shall pass. *So hang in there.* Let it ride regardless of its pain and duration.

Santa Claus Is Not Coming to Town

You did not live happily ever after. Your Prince Charming was the alias Prince Deceitful, and Little Bo Peep was not as innocent as you had believed, yet it still hurts. You were crushed when they finally told you that there was no Santa Claus, and even though your early childhood years were spent believing in a fantasy, for you, the illusion, like a dream at night, was for all intents and purposes a reality imprinted in your mind. Losing a loved one, like losing Kris Kringle, is parting with an illusion, a false hope or dream, and it is the return to reality that is so difficult to handle. You are back on your own now, the way your life used to be before the fairy tale began. The pains and hardships that you will be experiencing are the gaps that need to be filled, voids that existed long before your first telephone call or e-mail correspondence. Relationships can only fill so much of these voids. The rest is up to you.

Reality can be an unpleasant experience. It is certainly no mystery why people turn to drugs, alcohol and the television to avoid it. Nobody wants to embrace reality, and most of us do our best to try to deny, sugarcoat and avoid it, but resistance and denial are opiates that blind us to what it is that we really need to do to truly escape the uncomfortable situations in which we find ourselves (Lozoff). Both are akin to hope, which is typically likened to a carrot dangling in front of a horse's nose. They used to tell me in my college days back in Florida that the best cure for a hangover was more alcohol. A brief and intermittent high may indeed provide much needed comfort and balance in our lives of frequent stress, but we also need moments of sobriety. *We are healed of suffering only by experiencing it to the full,* asserted Marcel Proust. The only way out is through. Jack London once said that we cannot wait for inspiration but that we must go after it with a club. The same is true of bliss. We must first acknowledge our circumstances and situation, find out what needs to be done about it, and then do it. The more swiftly we face reality and make the necessary repairs, adjustments and adaptations, the sooner we will find relief. Hence, denial, avoidance and escape into the fantasy world of hallucinogens, stimulants, depressants, antidepressants, television and the Internet will be less compelling. We must also be realistic. We might not always get what we want when we want it. Life's schedule and plans for us are not always in accordance with our own (*Holy Bible* 591), but that is no reason to stop trying, for we have nothing to lose by pursuing and everything to gain.

Healing

"That should be the biggest problem you ever have," dad would say, and although he is probably right, the solution, however simple, is not quite so easy. You are not only grappling with a recent breakup but also with a lifetime of abandonment, hurt, insecurity, anger and guilt.

Shock and denial as well as depression, anger, guilt and a host of other emotional symptoms are typical reactions to loss and may leave you feeling stunned, dazed and disconnected from the world. Feelings may become intense and unpredictable, and you may experience extreme and rapid mood shifts. You may feel excessively anxious and insecure.

You may have repeated and vivid memories of the event, and flashbacks may occur suddenly, leaving you with anxiety and heart palpitations, so for the time being it would be best to avoid patronizing restaurants, shops and vacation spots where the two of you spent time together. Thinking, especially concentration, will be erratic. This is not the time to make major decisions. You can expect to lose or gain a significant amount of weight and endure many sleepless nights. Anniversaries and other reminders may trigger off upsetting memories. Relationships may become strained, especially if you become withdrawn. Isolation is the worst thing right now, and as difficult as it may be, you must make yourself available to the company of others. Reactions to trauma vary. Some slip immediately into depression while others experience an initial boost, followed by a delayed depressive episode, the duration and intensity depending upon the length and quality of the relationship, the circumstances, personality, sensitivity and background. Some people respond immediately while others have delayed reactions—sometimes months—or even years later. Some people push all of the wrong buttons, and if they exemplified a parent who had long since abandoned you, then you may relive the pain of rejection from someone of whom you have longed to gain love and approval. Physical or emotional trauma can lead to increased stress, depression, low self-esteem and *post-traumatic stress disorder* (an emotional state of discomfort and stress associated with the memories of a disturbing event). Other stressful situations that occur in the interim of your recovery will seem amplified and will elicit painful feelings and symptoms from your recent abandonment (APA).

In the meanwhile, make peace with the pain and the time that it will take to recover. Stick close to others, talk, express your feelings, attend support groups, and see a good therapist. Visit a psychiatrist, and take prescribed antidepressant medication if necessary. It may only be temporary, and it could save your life.

DEPRESSION

You are understandably feeling abysmally distraught, despondent and desperate. It hurts. Of course it hurts. It's supposed to hurt. You entrusted them with your heart and soul, which they kneaded, rolled, wrought, chewed up, spit out and trampled. You might as well have left your brand new convertible parked in front of an abandoned warehouse on a dark side street in New York City's Upper East Side or anywhere in Detroit. You may also have unresolved emotional and psychological issues that need to be addressed after all of these years.

Internalizing the rejection is natural, as are the pain and paralysis that accompany abandonment. The intensity of these feelings, however, is incumbent upon our self-concept.

Depression is intensified by poor self-esteem. Poor self-image leaves us questioning ourselves when we are abandoned. We fail to perceive *their* idiosyncrasies because we are so blinded by "ours." We take at face value anything that anybody says about us, positive or negative. Liking yourself minimizes depression and shame, but a poor self-concept, on the contrary, will undoubtedly intensify these intruders, even to fatal extremes (Linehan 108-10).

I know that each day I gradually become stronger, and one day I will have him only in my memories and not my heart. When that day comes, I know I will have made it through one of the hardest things in my lifetime. J. L. J.

In addition to therapy and supportive people in our lives, the following list may act as a guideline for developing self-esteem:

• *Accomplish*

The relationship has changed you. Trauma is changing you, and every day that passes you are continuing to change. You are becoming a better person–wiser, stronger, compassionate and mature. But maturity alone cannot bring happiness. You may find yourself spending much of your time alone and crying right now. It is extremely difficult to get up and go in the wake of a breakup. Nothing seems to give you any pleasure, not even sex. You may be finding yourself frustrated at not being able to enjoy the things that you once did, and if they were things that you did with your X, then they probably bring pain (Linehan 113).

It is critical that you discover and rediscover interests and passions within you at this time. Although your current state of mind may make it impossible to enjoy anything fully, they will provide a distraction and temporarily mitigate your pain. They will also, in addition to other factors, hasten your recovery as the void becomes filled with new and promising passions. You must do things that are going to make you feel good about life and about yourself (Linehan 116-18).

Short- and long-range goals and plans may have also been shattered as a result of this experience. Many of your dreams and hopes no doubt included the one who disappointed you, but as time goes on and you are pursuing new interests and pleasures, new goals and objectives will begin to arise, and you will have other things to which you can look forward, strive for and accomplish. With each hurdle and achievement, you will grow stronger, happier and more self-assured. Present day passions, plans, projections and accomplishments will play a major role in your recovery (Linehan 119). Keep busy. *There is no happiness without action*, declared Benjamin Disraeli. Set goals. Achieve goals. Said Thomas Carlyle, *nothing builds self-esteem and self-confidence like accomplishment.* Do things that make you feel competent and self-confident. You long for the past because you come up short in the present.

• *Trust yourself*

You're just as good as anyone else, dad always said. Your opinion is as valid as any other's. With low self-esteem, we fail to trust ourselves, to have faith in our own attitudes, opinions, actions and judgments. We feel as if we are alone and not entitled to assertions or stances as are others. We are often surprised when we are complimented or praised. Trust yourself. Have faith in yourself. Develop confidence in yourself through achievement.

• *Assert yourself*

You do not have to be aggressive to be assertive or confrontational to confront. "I felt a little hurt when you..." "Could I have handled that situation differently?" "I would really like to know what you thought about..." If you respect and take yourself seriously, then others will, too.

• *Appreciate yourself*

Are you a good friend? Are you conscientious and considerate? Do you try to do the right thing? Without self-esteem, we fail to recognize or appreciate our attributes, knowledge, experience and wisdom. Believing that we are lacking, we feel compelled to be perfect, to work harder than the average person, to perform better and to achieve more than everyone else just to *break even* with everyone else who *appears* to "have it all together."

• *Forgive yourself*

With a poor self-image, we tend to be overachievers, imposing stringent, sometimes impossible expectations upon ourselves. We project these self-imposed standards onto those around us, expecting them to be equally demanding. It is three strikes and we're out, and indeed, we are our own worst enemies and critics. Having a poor self-concept magnifies even the slightest breach of conduct while forgiving others for thoughts, words and behaviors far less forgivable. Is your guilt justified or irrational? *To err is human, to forgive divine*, said Alexander Pope. Only unforgiving and judgmental people cannot forgive others, and the unsound are devoid of any guilt, shame, remorse or conscience (Andreason).

• *Stop personalizing*

Stand aside from the situation. Step out of your spotlight. Stop amplifying all of your perceived misdoing. If you were able to acquire a large-scale or global perspective, then you would realize that you are only one insignificant microorganism on a vast orb of six and a half billion inhabitants, many of whom have committed far worse actions than you believe that you have.

A Necessary Evil

"Once you've moved on to bigger and better things, you look back and you realize that you enjoyed every moment of the struggle," consoled August Gunther to Ralph Kramden in a *Honeymooners* episode. Conflict is a necessary contrast to perfection. Imagine a world where everything you wanted was handed to you on a silver platter, every wish granted and each stride a breeze. There would be no goals to shoot for, no challenges and no obstacles to overcome. There would be nothing left to accomplish and nothing for which to look ahead and live. We would not learn or develop or have anything of value to offer the world.

Recall a *Twilight Zone* episode whereby a man was granted everything he wanted for all eternity only to find out that he was in Hell. In the 1950s, Yankee fans were actually getting bored watching their *Murderers Row* murder every opposing team in every championship year after year. When there is too much of a good thing, we lose our appreciation. Paul Pearsall even spoke of the depreciation of pleasure in excess and the danger of prolonged ecstasy (142). Is it not a gratifying experience to drink expensive wine out of an expensive goblet that you toiled, scrimped and saved to acquire? Even dining out can lose its flavor. Would you really appreciate a diploma or degree that had been handed to you, or can you look back with pride at the hard work, dedication and sleepless nights that you spent studying for exams and writing research reports? To this day, I refuse to install the new technologically advanced reeds in my bagpipes even though these small and convenient plastic miracles make playing less of an effort. One of the things that drew my interest in playing such a complicated musical instrument in the first place was the challenge that it presented. A good appetite makes food a feast, thirst turns water into a Cabernet, and bedtime is a paradise after a long, hard day on the job.

Once you have overcome your heartbreak and depression, you will be that much more appreciative and receptive to pleasures that you might have taken for granted previously. You will be more compassionate toward others. Many people who have undergone near-death experiences, for example, learn to find joy in simple things in life, such as a sunset or waking up to a new day.

As children, we bite our dentists, defy our teachers and complain about our parents only to look back with gratitude at all of the torment that they put us through for our own good. The spiritual speak of struggle as a necessary initiation into Self-realization. Siddhartha Gautama's life was exceedingly difficult prior to his enlightenment. The universe does not challenge the weak, and if you are faced with a difficult challenge, says inspirational speaker Les Brown, then the universe has respect for you. Brown brilliantly personifies life's trials as "whuppings" dealt to us by the universe, similar to the spanking that a young child might receive by a loving and concerned parent. This bitter medicine may not be ingested easily, but in the end, it proves to be a necessary stepping stone to a higher path. Bo Lozoff, author and renowned spiritual teacher and founder of the Human Kindness Foundation, likened suffering to a baby learning how to walk and an angel earning his wings. Friends say that whatever does not kill us makes us stronger. There is no gain without pain. Your pain may be your opponent now, but one day it will prove to have been your ally.

Dealing with Pain

Once life's knocked the wind out of you, Les Brown empathizes, *it's hard to pull yourself together. You feel empty, not yourself and you know it. Folks often describe this period in their life as purposeless, life having lost its luster.*

"Be strong!" they say. "Keep a stiff upper lip!" "Fight it!" In *We're All Doing Time*, Lozoff writes about a monk in Tibet who wished to meditate peacefully in a cave. Inside of the cave, however, lived several demons that enjoyed disturbing his meditations. At first, the monk tried to ignore them, hoping that they would leave. He then tried to drive them out with force, shouting at them and telling them to go away. This only made them more determined to agitate him. Realizing that it was futile to ignore or fight the demons, the monk decided that he had no other choice but to accept and coexist with them. The demons, seeing that they could trouble him no longer, finally flew away. Grief, pain, loneliness and fear cannot be fought or slain. They are invincible forces that come and go, and our only defense is openness and complete vulnerability. We must accept these demons and live with them. *Pain can never be conquered*, quoted Lozoff; *it's here to be endured like the sky endures a storm.* Your acceptance of your pain will relieve you of it, paradoxically. Thunderstorms leave rainbows in their wake. Better times are in store. God awards us the strength and fortitude that we need to endure difficult times and circumstances (Lozoff).

Be It Ever So Humble

It was a high counsel that I once heard given to a young person, 'Always do what you are afraid to do,' quoth Emerson. By resisting change, you may be letting yourself in for unhappy consequences. Change can be very uncomfortable and frightening. Your compulsion to return to your former partner may be a subconscious need to return "home," to the familiar, even if it is destructive. Your mate might have provided security, structure, discipline and a groove as well as companionship, and now it feels as if you have been thrown out of your home and into the cold night air. Ironically, however, you are returning home. It is just that you have been away for so long that you are feeling anxious and confused. You are experiencing a readjustment period similar to what you felt when you returned home from being away at school or camp. You may have outgrown many interests and former aspects of yourself. You will probably make new friends and lose some old friends. Do not resist the changes that are occurring within you. They are steering you in the right direction. This is a period of rediscovery, of redefinition, of trial and error and of learning. It is the first day of the rest of your life. You are starting over, wearing out a new groove.

A New Life

"Just after my breakup, I left Virginia to make a fresh start in New York," Toni disclosed. Wipe the slate clean. When you are ready, make new plans. Set new goals and projections. Have new expectations. During times such as these, many people change jobs and careers and move to new places. Do not make any rash decisions, however, without thinking them through very carefully, for during times such as these, our minds tend to think irrationally. *Sometimes you have to take some chances*, continues Brown. *Sometimes you have to move on and not even know where you're going, but you've got to go*. Victor Frankyl maintained that what we need in fact is not a tensionless state but rather the striving and struggling for a goal worthy of us, that is, a suitable challenge tailored right to our needs and abilities to meet that engagement.

When I'm Sixty-Four

I hold it true, what'er befall; I feel it, when I sorrow most, Tis better to have loved and lost than never to have loved at all. See yourself at sixty-four or older, looking back. In all likelihood, your biggest regrets would be not having had experienced love and companionship, taken more risks, enjoyed more or having been good to yourself. Just consider this perspective the next time that you regret having met this person, having had your heart broken or the next time that you are reluctant to buy yourself that expensive item, make that big move or decision or do those things that you never thought you would–or could. *In the end,* cited Lincoln, *it is not the years in your life that count but the life in your years.* Although you may not agree with Tennyson right now, one day when you are older, looking back, you will be able to say that you did have that opportunity and experience at least once in life.

Yes Virginia, Time Really Does Heal All Wounds!

From the moment it is planted, the Chinese Bamboo Tree can take close to five years to begin to germinate, illustrated Les Brown, *but once it does, it can sprout and grow up to ninety feet in five weeks. Did it take five weeks for the tree to grow or five years?* Likewise, we are healing with each passing moment, though it may not seem so. Recovery is being nurtured and cultivated. Those who plant the seeds of the tree can do no more than keep watering it until it does make that rapid progression. Similarly, a series of what appear to be small steps can suddenly accelerate into rapid strides. On a "feeling-good" scale of one to ten, you may perpetuate a one or a five for as long as three years and then make a rapid jump to a seven or higher. It is ludicrous for one who sows to stand watch over his plot of land every day waiting for the first visible signs of germination that will not occur for at least four years; however, he knows that the tree's growth is forthcoming and can rest in the knowledge and assurance of this. Losing weight can likewise seem an eternity if we bow to our scales every hour on the hour. We must remember that healing and happiness, though not immediate, is forthcoming.

There is a light at the end of the tunnel, and this too shall pass.

"I'll never board another plane again!" you promised yourself and others. "You'll never live that down," they assured you. "I'll never speak to him again!" "This is definitely my last drink!" Are you still plagued by difficult events that occurred many years ago? Perhaps what was once an acute emotional pain is now a dull, chronic ache. Likewise, heartbreak is mitigated and eventually released through time and process. Like a furious tempest that wreaks its mighty force, it ultimately dissipates over time. What seems an eternity now shall wither into oblivion.

Every action has an equal and opposite reaction. There is a time to mourn and a time to dance. Nothing dries sooner than a tear. All emotions are temporary. Nothing stays the same. Dr. Pearsall theorizes that emotional reactions to a stimulus are followed automatically by an opposite or opponent reaction. Repeat exposures to an emotional stimulus will cause the initial reaction to weaken and the opponent process that follows to be stronger. Built into our nature is a protective compensatory system which promises that no matter how low we get, we will also get that high, and that the longer we are high or low the less intense these states become (Pearsall 206+). Thus, confirms Proverbs, *Even in laughter the heart is sad and the end of joy is grief* (*Holy Bible* 903). Urges and feelings do not last forever. There is an end in sight. Feeling is healing; it just takes time.

Planting the Seeds

Respect your values and beliefs. Act in ways that make you feel moral and virtuous. Do things that make you feel capable and effective. Accept praise and reject put downs. Seek out honest, sincere, kind and compassionate people (Pearsall 142).

Do not submit to erroneous myths and distorted viewpoints. You have a right to your thoughts, feelings and attitudes. Look around you. Other people's assertions are no more valid than yours. If someone gets upset with you, it does not mean that it is your fault.

You are allowed to be wrong, to make mistakes and to say and do outrageous things. S/he did. It is okay to break down, to cry and to be "weak." There is nothing wrong with seeking support and help from others, especially now. You would have been there for them. The only thing wrong is your perception.

Do not do anything that will bring you harm. Channel your pain, sorrow and anger into something gainful and productive. Jot down your thoughts and feelings in a diary. Be your own therapist. Feel your feelings. Observe your thoughts. Trace them. Understand them. Introspection or the investigation and inquiry into the nature of our thoughts, feelings, attitudes and behaviors is a component of yoga study and indeed with other Eastern practices (Hittleman). Win. Success is the sweetest revenge. Suicide is cutting the nose to spite the face, as well as a person who has about as much compassion as Adolph Hitler, Joseph Stalin or a New York City civil service employee. It is a permanent solution to a temporary problem and will only destroy the lives of those who really do care–in addition to your own.

Soothe yourself with psalms and proverbs of truth and wisdom. Trust God. Blame God. Everything happens for a reason. Everything happens for the best. Rest in trust, rest in the bigness and in the grand scheme (Lozoff). You may not like what has happened, but it could turn out to be the best thing that ever did happen, a blessing in disguise. Create mantras. Write them down on post-its. See them everywhere you go: the bathroom, the refrigerator, the car, the desk, the phone, everywhere you can. Repeat them. Reinforce them.

THERAPY

Do not feel too proud to seek counseling. Do not be shocked that you find yourself in need of it. It is nothing of which to feel ashamed. It does not make you weak. Find yourself a competent and caring therapist. If the therapist whom you meet sounds more like a businessman than a counselor, then you will know where his or her heart really lies. If s/he seems more like a timekeeper for a basketball game, then you need to bounce them and move on to a better coach. Your analyst should be patient and committed and not quick to commit you as a patient. He has confidence in his clients.

In treatment, the patient reveals all thoughts as they occur through *free association*. The patient and the analyst attempt to understand the psychological meaning of the ideas, fantasies, dreams and behaviors that are expressed. Your therapist should be an individual who listens, understands, empathizes, supports, encourages and validates you (Narcotics Anonymous).

A good therapist listens. He returns your phone calls and does not tell you that you are abusing the "privilege" or that he "has a life, too." A dedicated psychologist will neither cut you off in mid sentence because your time is up, nor will she reverse the charges on the return phone call. He will not charge you a session or suggest an extra one because your phone conversation exceeded five minutes. A good therapist supports you. He is more interested in your recovery than in your insurance co-payment. An enormous clock does not obscure your view of her, nor does she have a taxicab meter within her reach. You want her to call to say, "Is everything OK?" and not, "I'm raising my fee." A conscientious and confident analyst will not tell you how bad you are and how good *he* is. He believes in you. He has confidence in you. He trusts you. He accentuates your attributes. She focuses on the positive.

Recovery

You will know that your recovery is on the mend when you no longer take all of the blame for every misfortunate incident that befalls you and those around you, when you no longer permit yourself to be manipulated, used and controlled, and when out of loneliness or fear of being alone, you stop settling for people who fall far short of your standards and expectations.

You will know that your self-acceptance is on the rise when what you think, feel, say and do are not determined by others' attitudes and actions or what you perceive them to be. When you are able to identify and express as well as avoid minimizing all of your thoughts, feelings and attitudes, whether they be anger or serenity; sorrow as well as joy; hate as well as love; jealousy as well as support; apathy as well as interest; surprise; guilt and shame, then you will have attained a higher level of self-respect. You will know that you are finally starting to accept yourself when you are no longer ashamed or judgmental of your thoughts or emotions, labeling them as weak or strong, and when you are no longer fearful of being emotionally honest with others and yourself. You will know that you are awakening in the recovery room when you are able to release the self-induced need for destructive self-criticism.

You will reap the benefits of self-esteem when you are free to be and do as you are without the perpetual fear of criticism and disapproval. You will begin to appreciate yourself when you can value your own opinions, when you can allow yourself to fall short of perfection and when you can acknowledge your attributes and assets and praise yourself for the things that you do, think and say, knowing that you are good enough and no longer judging yourself by *their* standards.

You will know that your self-confidence has returned when you are no longer crippled by your fear of risk and when you start going out and following your fancy, for the person who risks nothing does nothing and has nothing *is* nothing, and though he may avoid suffering and sorrow, he will not feel, grow, love and live. True happiness and self-esteem will come not only from mere praise but by embracing, grappling with and surmounting each challenge and obstacle that comes your way.

You gain strength, courage, and confidence by every experience in which you really stop to look fear in the face, believed Eleanor Roosevelt. *You must do the thing which you think you cannot do.* Make it your business and your goal in life to meet challenge after challenge; struggle after struggle; obstacle after obstacle and goal after goal. Live one moment at a time. Pat yourself on the back, and be proud for having the valor to pursue your dreams. Struggle, and how we respond to it, is our path to self-discovery. *The harder the battle, the sweeter the victory* (Brown).

When it is dark enough, you can see the stars.

Ralph Waldo Emerson

The Process of Progress

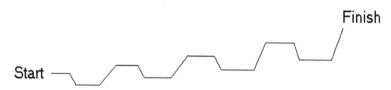

A common misconception is that individuals who suffer from heartbreak and depression can simply put it all behind them if they choose. This might be true for the indifferent; however, for people who have the capacity to love, this is simply not the case. What these philosophers and counselors fail to understand is that letting go is a process not any different from learning. I know of a therapist who told his former client that all she had to do to feel good again was to "let go" of the man who hurt her, one week after lecturing her about the steps involved in the grieving process. Eventually one does reach the point where she or he can say, "I no longer choose to be hurt by this person" and actually does it, but getting to this point of readiness is a long time coming. It takes time, but it does happen, whether it is getting over a loss, pursuing a passion, materializing money or accomplishing a goal. The problem is in assuming that everything be over and done yesterday. Those kinds of unreasonable expectations set us up for anxiety, disappointment and discouragement. Waiting for results can seem an eternity if we neglect living. Things usually happen when we are not thinking about them, when we are not waiting in anticipation for the Heinz Ketchup to pour. Plant the seeds of the goal or wish the first year, watch it sprout the second, and see it fully grown in the third. By

The path to our destination is not always a straight one.

Barbara Hall

the fourth or fifth year, you shall be enjoying the fruits of your labor.

Accomplishment may be the single best medicine and source of relief in the midst of depression. Despite your most valiant efforts, you may not be able to achieve detachment right now, six months from now or even three years from now no matter how much you try to dupe yourself into believing that it no longer affects you, but eventually with time and achievement, you shall.

The Start of a Beautiful Friendship

Of my friends, I am the only one I have left, said Heauton Timorumenos Terence. Appreciate yourself. Impress yourself. Impress others. Discover passions. Entertain yourself. Make plans. Make projections. Set goals. Give yourself three to five years for meeting these goals. For now, what would bring you some solace, comfort and joy? What would fill the void? You have been hurt. When you were a child, your mother or father might have treated you to a candy bar or an ice cream cone after that traumatic experience at the dentist's office, taken you out for lunch following that painful injection or blood test at the hospital or bought you a new toy when other hardships or disappointments befell you. In the 1991 box office hit *Arthur,* Hobson suggests that Arthur treat himself to two dozen sweaters instead of the one dozen that he had originally planned to purchase, to soothe his friend who is angry and upset at his father for trying to control his life. What will be your two dozen sweaters, ice cream cone, candy bar or toy? Frank found his solace through other people, through support groups. The pen aided William during his difficult time. Kevin turned to karaoke. Jane finds pleasure in reading. Mitch works overtime and keeps a saturated schedule. Franco spends much of his time with his art, paying close attention to detail, as does Mick with his model airplanes. Blake is a kung fu devotee. Madison has her acting and her dancing. Randy finds his pleasure in baking, and Paula finds hers in her children. Lisa and Scott enjoy their house in Florida and their outdoor Jacuzzi. Steve enjoys his Harley. Many people, such as Christine, turn to the Church. Many folks escape to the movies.

As we recover, many of our old "demons" will come back to haunt us. Life may again become meaningless, monotonous and boring. We may encounter old foes such as apathy and procrastination, fear and insecurity, but these are often the periods of our greatest growth. We recover in peaks and valleys. Meanwhile, we are healing with every setback, whether it feels so or not. A throbbing wound is also a healing wound. The mind is setting itself for its next leap forward. We may grow emotionally and physically exhausted, yet true conversion deep within may be giving us the answers that alter our inner motivations and change our lives. "It may take a while, but you'll figure yourself out," the occupational therapist tells Henry who is recovering from amnesia because of a gunshot wound in Mike Nichols's *Regarding Henry*. Much awaits you.

How Doth the Little Busy Bee?

Repression is not the most desirable method of mitigating the pain of the memory of a lost one, for it fuels distorted memory as well as guilt and needless self-deprecation (Miracosta). Therefore, allow it to dissolve through distraction. Keep busy, very busy. Get a calendar book. Fill it up. There are 86, 400 seconds in a day. Account for each one of them. Plan and structure your day the night before. Know exactly what you are going to do that day, every hour on the hour, and since you probably will not be getting much sleep for a while anyway, you can plan to be busy for each and every second each day.

Go to church. Get involved with a committee.

Work two jobs–three jobs.

If you cannot sleep, get up. Clean the apartment. Go shopping. Patronize the all-night supermarkets for those nights of insomnia or bad dreams. If you have friends who live in another time zone, then you can call them when it is daytime there and after hours here.

Stay out of the house. Leave your apartment earlier for work, and have breakfast at the local diner or coffee shop. Plan to eat dinner out as well. It does not have to be an elaborate or expensive restaurant; even the neighborhood Chinese takeout place or pizzeria would suffice.

Keep a journal. Read books that will inspire you and quell your pain.

Buy yourself an entire DVD or VHS collection of your favorite movies and television episodes (none should have any association with your former companion).

Try all of those things that you used to fantasize about but thought that you would never do. Take flying lessons–if you are not taking Prozac. Study a musical instrument. Learn karate, box, and take up judo, tae kwon do or some other mind-engaging physical activity.

You need a challenge right now. *Happiness is activity*, preached Aristotle. Plan ahead and make projections. Accomplish. Plan, project and accomplish again. Do not stay idle. Idleness breeds grief and despair.

From morning's first light
Till the coming of night,
He's singing and toiling
The summer day through.
Oh! We may get weary,
And think work is dreary;
'Tis harder by far
To have nothing to do.

Marian Douglas

THE SPIRIT OF X MAS

THE CITY STREETS WERE WHITE WITH SNOW. BRIGHT LIGHTS EMANATED FROM THE RETAIL AND SPECIALTY SHOPS, SETTING THE OTHERWISE DARKENED STREETS AGLOW. EVEN THE LATENESS OF THE HOUR DID NOT PREVENT THE RUSH OF SHOPPERS HUSTLING IN AND OUT OF THE DEPARTMENT STORES. HOLIDAY MUSIC FILLED THE AIR, AS DID THE BELLS AND CHIMES, WHICH WOULD ALSO PAVE THE WAY FOR THE NEW YEAR. GREAT CROWDS FILLED THE STREETS OF NEW YORK CITY'S BROADWAY AND HERALD SQUARE WHILE RAPIDLY FORMING LINES OF SHIVERING PATRONS STOOD OUTSIDE PATIENTLY AWAITING SHOWS AND MUSICALS. CHRISTMAS TREES OF ALL SIZES WERE BEING SOLD TO AVID AND EAGER PATRONS WHO WOULD HURRY HOME TO ADORN THEM. NONE OF COURSE COULD COMPETE WITH THE GREAT BIG TREE IN MIDTOWN ATTRACTING PASSIONATE SPECTATORS FROM AS FARAWAY AS CALIFORNIA. EXCITED CHILDREN EAGERLY ANTICIPATED THE HOLIDAY GIFTS THEY HAD WAITED FOR ALL YEAR. THEY PLAYED HAPPILY IN THE DEEP, COTTONY MOUNDS OF SNOW, GROOVING ANGEL FIGURES, BUILDING SNOW MEN AND SNOW CASTLES FROM WHERE THEY WOULD LAUNCH THEIR SNOWBALLS DURING THEIR SNOWBALL FIGHTS WITH THEIR FRIENDS. INSIDE THE HOMES, FROSTY, RUDOLPH, THE GRINCH AND THE PEANUTS WERE BEING BROADCAST TO FAMILIES WHILE SNOWMEN, REINDEER AND SANTA FIGURES STOOD GUARD IN THE BARRENLY COLD OUTSIDE. THE AROMA OF FRESHLY COOKED TURKEYS AND HAMS, AS WELL AS AN ASSORTMENT OF MOUTH-WATERING BAKED PIES, CAKES AND PASTRIES ENVELOPED THE AIR IMMEDIATELY OUTSIDE WHILE DELIGHTING THE FRIENDS AND FAMILIES INSIDE WHO WOULD SHARE IN FABULOUS FOOD AND DRINK! CHILDREN WERE CAROLING. ADULTS WERE SHOUTING, "A MERRY CHRISTMAS TO ALL!"

Holly Days vs. Holy Days

Fa, la, la, la, la, la, la, la, la. Santa, Bloomingdale's, Macy's, Radio City Musical Hall, Rockefeller Center, The Brady Bunch–it is enough to make you want to jump down your chimney without care. Even Midnight Mass becomes just another festivity for most of its congregation who will probably not set foot inside of a church again until the following Christmas Eve. Fr. M. from my seminary days once delivered a brilliant homily one holiday season, distinguishing Christmas–the "idea"–from Christmas–the meaning. The Peanuts's Linus delivered a profound sermon of his own.

Christ's Mass

When this time of year brings you down, remember the *true* meaning of Christmas as opposed to the true meaning of commercialism subtly illustrated in the short literary description on the previous page, and the true meaning of Christmas can be summed up in one Word–Christ (Merriam-Webster Collegiate Dictionary 11: 220). Anything beyond that is not Christmas but merely hype to the delight of profiting businesses and added sorrow to the already forlorn. It is not Christmas or Hanukkah, per se, that is so depressing; it is the commercialism. Christ did not intend for people to lament over the memories of shopping, feasting and Broadway shows. If you really want to observe the holidays, then read some spiritual literature. Learn the origins of Chanukah, Kwanza and Eid. Give the most precious gifts of all–love and kindness–and keep Christ, Moses, Buddha, Mohammed and other prophets and saints of the ages close to your heart. There are a number of religious sects that do not celebrate the holidays at all.

Chestnuts roasting on an open fire, Santa Claus coming to town, Rudolph the red-nosed reindeer, presents-as adults we need to put this time of year into a rational, mature, adult perspective. Elves do not exist, deer do not fly, and I have never been able to figure out how Santa can cover the entire globe in one night when it takes American Airlines close to six hours on a direct flight from New

York to Los Angeles. Tune out the tunes, do not look into the lights, and do not expect Santa Claus to come down your chimney, if you have one. Lower your expectations, and do not let the holiday spirit worsen yours.

And the angel said to them, "Be not afraid; for behold, I bring you good news of a great joy which will come to all the people; for to you is born this day in the city of David a Savior, who is Christ the Lord. And this will be a sign for you: you will find a babe wrapped in swaddling cloths and lying in a manger." And suddenly there was with the angel a multitude of the heavenly host praising God and saying, "Glory to God n the highest, and on earth peace among men with whom he is pleased!"

Luke 2:10-14

Chapter Summary
…To the Dawn of Discovery

Be strong! I know it's hard. You just hang in there.
"Stronger Each Day" is our motto.
Janie Logan--Jones

You shall get through this. Pain is temporary. Time gives us a gift at the end of our suffering similar to the rainbow that an awesome thunderstorm leaves in its wake. After the feeling comes the healing (Brown). There will be a time, but it shall be of time's choosing and not yours (*Holy Bible* 903). Recovery is not an overnight process. There are no six–month-to-one–year guarantees, quick remedies, instant repair manuals or ancient Chinese secrets. Friends, family and words of wisdom may provide relief and accumulate over time to hasten your recovery, but change takes time and action. Nothing worthwhile comes easy. You may not notice, but your wound is healing. "We wish we could rush it," my friend Janie would say, "but time heals all wounds; the heart one just takes longer."

In the meantime, make each moment count. Meet each hurdle. Think positive. Trust yourself. Look ahead. Pursue your passions. Achieve your goals. An inverted glass will not take water. The only one who can stop you is you. Keep your mind filled with good thoughts about yourself, pleasant dreams, and make them a reality.

He was full of ennui, full of misery, full of death; there was nothing left in the world that could attract him, that could give him pleasure and solace. There was no more purpose. Siddhartha was horrified. He was lost, confused, so devoid of all reason, that he had sought death...

Siddhartha

...I had to experience nausea and the depths of despair in order to learn not to resist them, in order to learn to love the world, and no longer compare it with some kind of desired imaginary vision of perfection, but to leave it as it is, to love it and be glad to belong to it.

**Weeping may tarry
for the night,
but joy comes with the
morning.**

Psalms 30:5

CONCLUSION

...To Discovery

CONCLUSION... To Discovery

She found an infinite number of reasons why a relationship with you would not work. He failed to nurture your identity. She challenged your integrity and fostered insecurity. Everything that you did annoyed him, and nothing ever pleased her. Understanding that it is the displacement of unresolved conflicts, dependencies and aggressions onto a substitute object that accounts for repeated mismatches, you chose to take responsibility for allowing this individual into your life and pledged never to repeat unhealthy relationship choices.

At the attrition of our own esteem, we respected, empowered and esteemed an individual who did not merit such admiration or returned it but reciprocated with disdain and deceit. Giving them the best of who we are, we tried in vain to win the love and approval of someone who did not acknowledge, appreciate or even realize who we are and what we offered. Given our conscientious natures, our need to self-recriminate, our lack of self-esteem, our need to be perfect and our contorted idealistic perception of those who abandoned us, we personalized the rejection, blamed ourselves and neglected to recognize our attributes and the assets that we brought into the relationship.

It is often the worst events in our lives that turn out to be the best things that ever happen to us; thus, we considered the long-term consequences and problems that might have ultimately manifested had we remained with this individual. Outcomes and other peoples' behaviors are not usually within our control or within the confines of our expectations and imaginations.

Rest assured that you are not alone. Others are suffering the pain that you are and worse. Others have been hurt and tossed aside, too, and they all share the same thoughts, questions and feelings that you and I do. What went wrong? What did I do?

You shall get there. Positive people; support groups; a therapist; a priest; minister; rabbi or shaykh; family; compassionate, caring and wise friends–these are the people who are going to get you through when others and yourself have lost patience and given up. Do not go it alone. Like the therapist, your support network should be friends who can listen patiently and empathize with you. If they are not sympathetic or fail to support or respect your feelings in any way, then it would be advisable for you to turn to people who will. The best ears may turn out to be strangers, coworkers, childhood friends or acquaintances whom you least expected to come to your aid. Reach out. Do not suffer in silence.

It is past hurts for which we carry the perpetual burden and project onto those who have wronged us in the present. Since we cannot hope to avenge ourselves of the villains from the past, our only hope of salvation in the present is to forgive those who have brought us great suffering, both then and now.

"There are things that you have to do battle against," says Bo Lozoff. The only way out of our pain is to experience it to the fullest and wait patiently for it to run its course similar to the newborn infant who needs to cry out the emotional and physical trauma experienced during the prenatal phase of his life. The kind and loving parent who interferes with this emotional release by patronizing the baby is merely perpetuating it. It is necessary for the tear to run its cycle. Says Geneen Roth, *Healing is the intermediate step between grieving and growing. The purpose of healing is to become whole and the reason for becoming whole is to move ahead toward a vision of life in which you are fully alive, connected to what sustains you and available to receive and give love* (Primal Page). We are also aware that it is during this painful healing time that we can trace the origin of our pain through an understanding of some psychology-based principles, and through psychoanalysis, rediscover ourselves as we continue to live our lives, seek out new experiences and new people and develop a more positive sense of self through focusing on our attributes and our passions, confronting fear, taking risks and accomplishing our goals and projections with reasonable expectations. It is usually during times such as these that we are likely to effect some much needed changes that we have neglected to make out of fear and the need for "security."

We are not going to be stagnant. The new courses for which we set sail might not always take us to the Promised Land right away, but with inaction, we shall surely sink. Remember, you are not a loser because you fail; you are a success because you try. Without struggle, our lives would be about as exciting as a stop at a red traffic light. There would be no purpose. Be patient and give it time.

Make peace with the pain and the time that it will take for recovery. Accept it. By thinking about them every five seconds today when yesterday it might have been every four seconds, even if you gain one second each day, you are making progress. Accept that this is where you are at this time of your life right now.

It is about time. Loss, death, injury–you have been through trauma before. You know that time mitigates the pain and decreases the frequency and duration of thoughts and associations. Be patient. Everything changes; nothing stays the same. Where there is sadness, happiness is waiting right around the corner. So take heart and be of good cheer, for the best is yet to come!

Closing Statement

You gave it your best. You have done everything that you could to save the relationship. He knows that you love him. She knows that you cared. You have nothing to be sorry about and nothing to feel guilty about. He knows that the door is open. If for whatever reasons he had, who you are and what you had to offer were not good enough, then so be it. Sooner or later time will feed it all back to them. Let *him* regret it. Let *her* feel guilty. They too must live with the hurt that they caused you. Let *him* miss the good times, and let her miss *you*. Time will tell just how important you were.

Eventually this tenacious grip shall lose its hold on you. Cure will occur when you have felt and received insight into a particular pain enough to be able to change the situation in the present that keeps triggering that pain. How long it will take is impossible to say, but it does come to an end. Benjamin Franklin said that time is an herb that cures all diseases. Sometimes you just have to wait a little while. Time is the greatest healer and experience–the greatest teacher. You have suffered a defeat, a set back, a crushing blow to your dignity and your integrity.

Bide your time and hang in there. It is rough, it is painful and it is stormy, but everything shall fall into place. Until then, live, learn and grow. Make your life as comfortable and as pleasant for yourself as possible, and let this guide be your companion along the way. I survived this, and you shall, too. All my best!

You spot a lighthouse afar in a storm
  out at sea.
No matter how stormy the weather
  may be,
No matter how turbulent the sea,
No matter how fierce the raging
  winds,
    and threatening the swells may be,

You stand alone, brave sea
  captain, against a formidable foe,
Fearful of the wrath of the thunder
  up high;
Stricken with terror by the white
  blazing sky,
    and smitten in the face by the
    blustery winds.

Blinded by the torrents of rain
   with eyes squinted tight,
You keep your eyes on that
beacon of light.
For it is a promise;
   the end is in sight.

Though this tempest be long,
   and it seems so my friend,
I've yet to see a storm
   that did not come to an end.

The Author

Works Cited

AllButForgottenOldies.net. 2002-2004. All But Forgotten Oldies.net. Web. 22 Aug. 2004.

AllWatchers.com. Web. 12 Dec. 2004.

Amazon.com. Amazon.com Co. Web. 9 July 2004.

Anderson, Ken. *Where to Find It in the Bible*. Nashville: Thomas Nelson, Inc. 1996. Print.

Andreasen, Nancy C. "Mental Illness." *World Book Online Reference Center*. Feb. 2004. World Book, Inc. Web. 1 Feb. 2004.

AOL Movies. 1999-2004. AOL Movies. Web. 22 Nov. 2004.

APA.org. March 2002. Web. 13 July 2004.

Arthur. Dir. Steve Gordon. Perf. Dudley Moore, Liza Minnelli, Stephen Elliott, and Sir John Gielgud. Robert Greenhut, 1981. Film.

Baker, Lyman. *Lyman A. Baker*. 30 Apr. 2000. Web. 27 June 2004.

Barnes & Noble, Inc. *The Aesop for Children*. Hong Kong: Barnes & Noble Books, 1993. Print.

Beatles Greatest Hits Vol. 2 for Guitar. New York: ATV Music Publications, 1980. Print.

Borden, Lee. *Divorceinfo.com*. 1996-2004. Divorceinfo.com. Web. 27 June 2004.

BrainyQuote.com. 2004. BrainyMedia.com. Web. 27 June 2004.

Brown, Les. *Choosing Your Future*. Les Brown Enterprises, LLC. Audiocassette.

Buss, Arnold H. *Psychology: Behavior in Perspective*. Austin: John Wiley and Son, 1978. Print.

Caringonline.com. Web. 1 Jul. 2004.

CharacterProducts.com. 2000-2004. Character Products, Inc. Web. 10 July 2004.

Civprod.com. Web. 4 Dec. 2004.

CliffsNotes.com. 2000-2005. Wiley Publishing, Inc. Web. 4 Mar 2005.

Co-Dependents Anonymous: Members and Sponsors. Interviews & Correspondence *Co-Dependents Anonymous*. 15 Aug. 2002-15 May 2003. Print.

Co-Dependents Anonymous, Inc. *Being in a Dependent Relationship*. Dallas: Core Publications, 1995. Print.

Co-Dependents Anonymous, Inc. *Co-Dependency and Recovery-A Comparison* Dallas: Core Publications, 1995. Print.

Co-Dependents Anonymous, Inc. *Recovery: How Will I Know?* Dallas: Core Publications, 1995. Print.

Works Cited

Co-Dependents Anonymous, Inc. *The Patterns of Codependency* Dallas: Core
    Publications, 1995. Print.

Co-Dependents Anonymous, Inc. *What Is Codependence?* Dallas: Core Publications, 1995. Print.

CompuServe.com. Web. 20 Jan. 2004.

Cool Quotes.com. Web. 7 Aug. 2004.

CyberMontana.com. Web. 7 Nov 2004.

Daily Script.com. Web. 12 Dec. 2004.

"Deciding Vote, The." *The Honeymooners*. Dumont Electronicam T-V Film System. Jackie
    Gleason Enterprises, Inc. Productions Park Sheraton Hotel, New York City, NY Dec. 1955.
    Television.

Divorcereform.org. Web. 27 June 2004.

DivorceMagazine.com. 1996-2004. Segue Esprit, Inc. Web. 13 July 2004.

DocumentsandDesigns.com. 2002. Terri@Documents and Designs.Com. Web. 13 July 2004.

"Domestic Violence." *World Book Online Reference Center*. 2004. World Book, Inc. Web. 18
    Feb. 2004.

Douglas, Marian. "The Song of the Bee." *Online Poems*. Web. 15 Nov. 2007.

Dressed to Kill. Dir. Brian De Palma. Perf. Michael Caine, Angie Dickinson, Nancy Allen, Dennis
    Franz, and Keith Gordon. MGM, 1980. Film.

Dyer, Wayne Dr. *Pulling Your Own Strings*. New York: HarperCollins, 2001. Print.

Easy Guitar: BEATLEMANIA, 1963-1966. New York: Warner Bros. Publications, Inc., 1978. Print.

ElayneSavage.com. 2003. Web. 16 Aug. 2004.

Elyrics4You.com. 2000-2004. Elyrics4u.com. Web. 11 July 2004.

Entplaza.com. 2001-2003. Entplaza.com. Web. 27 June 2004.

2FamousLyrics.com. Web. 27 June 2004.

Famous Quotes and Famous Sayings Network. 1994-2004. Web. 22 Aug. 2004.

Felluga, Dino. "Modules on Freud: Transference and Trauma." *Introductory Guide to Critical
    Theory*. 28 Nov., 2003. Purdue U. Web. 12 Feb., 2004.

Felluga, Dino. "Terms Used by Psychoanalysis." *Introductory Guide to Critical Theory*. 28
    Nov., 2003. Purdue U. Web. 12 Feb., 2004.

FitzMaurice, Kevin Everette. *KevinFitzMaurice.com*. 2002-2004. Web. 19 Aug. 2004.

Works Cited

"Forget." *Merriam-Webster Online Dictionary*. 2004. Merriam-Webster, Inc. Web. 18 Feb. 2004.

Frances, Allen. "Psychoanalysis." *World Book Online Reference Center*. Feb. 2004. World Book, Inc. Web. 1 Feb. 2004.

Franklin, Benjamin. *Poor Richard's Almanack*. Ed. Paul Leicester Ford. New York: Peter Pauper Press. Print.

Freedman, Russell. *Confucious: The Golden Rule*. New York: Scholastic, Inc., 2002. Print.

"Friend." *Webster's New World Dictionary and Thesaurus: Second Edition*. Hungry Minds, Inc. New York. 2002. Print.

Friends General Conference. *Friends and Weddings*. Philadelphia: FGC, 1989. Print.

Frost, Robert. "The Road Not Taken." *Bartleby.com*. Web. 27 June 2004.

Gaudette, Pat. "Divorce Support: Abusive Relationships-More about Abuse." *About.com*. About, Inc., 2004. Web. 18 Feb. 2004.

Gaudette, Pat. "Divorce Support: Verbal Abuse." *About.com*. About, Inc., 2004. Web. 18 Feb. 2004.

Geometcalf.com. Web. 1 Feb. 2004.

Glut, Donald F. "The Empire Strikes Back." *Star Wars: The Star Wars Trilogy*. The Ballantine Publishing Group. New York: Ballantine Books, 1980. Print.

"Golden Man, The." *Lost in Space*. An Irwin Allen Production. Twentieth Century-Fox. Television, Inc., CBS Television Network, Hollywood, CA 28 Dec. 1966. Television.

Greenburg, Dan. *HOW TO MAKE YOURSELF MISERABLE*. New York: Random House. Print.

Hay, Louise. *You Can Heal Your Life*. Carlsbad: Hay House, 1999. Print.

Heartbreak Kid, The. Dir. Elaine May. Perf. Charles Grodin, and Cybill Shepherd. Anchor Bay Ent., 1972. Film.

Heartquotes.net. 2003. Heartmath, LLC. Web. 13 July 2004.

Henderson, Charles. "Christianity-General: The Meaning of Forgiveness in a World of War." *About.com*. About, Inc., 2004. Web. 18 Feb. 2004.

Henderson, Charles. "Christianity-General: The Parable of the Unforgiving Servant: A Contemporary Paraphrase." *About.com*. About, Inc., 2004. Web. 18 Feb. 2004.

Hesse, Hermann. *Siddhartha*. New York: New Directions Publishing Corporation, 1951. Print.

Hittleman, Richard. *The Problem, the Solution*. Steve Mark Harris/Clear Lake Productions, 1989. Audiocassette.

Works Cited

Hittleman, Richard. *Yoga Meditation.* Clear Lake Productions/Steve Mark Harris Productions, Inc., Santa Cruz, CA. Audiocassette.

Hittleman, Richard. *Yoga Workshop Lectures.* Steve Mark Harris/Clear Lake Productions, 1991. Videocassette.

Holy Bible. Nashville: Holman Bible Publishers, 1982. Print.

Holy Bible, The. New American Catholic Edition. New York: Benziger Brothers, Inc., 1961. Print.

Holy Bible, The. New York: Watchtower Bible and Tract Society, Inc., 1929. Print.

Home Data West. Web. 2 Feb. 2004.

Home.Tiscali.Be. 6 Mar. 1997. Behavior Profiling. Web. 19 Nov. 2004.

HometownCompanion.com. Web. 11 July 2004.

Imdb.com. 1990-2004. Internet Movie Database, Inc. Web. 9 Jul. 2004.

"I Will Survive." Gloria Gaynor. Comp. By Dino Fekaris and Freddie Perren. 1979. Print.

Jesus of Nazareth. Dir. Franco Zeffirelli. Perf. Robert Powell, Michael York, Sir Laurence Olivier, James Earl Jones, Anne Bancroft, Olivia Hussey, Rod Steiger, Anthony Quinn, Christopher Plummer, and Ernest Borgnine. NBC TV, 1977. Television.

Johnson, David, ed. *InfoPlease.com.* 2000-2003. Pearson Education. Web. 27 June 2004.

Katz, Nikki. "Women's Issue: Domestic Violence Statistics." *About.com.* About, Inc. Web. 18 Feb. 2004.

"Keeper, The." *Lost in Space.* An Irwin Allen Production. Twentieth Century-Fox Television, Inc., CBS Television Network, Hollywood, CA. 12 Jan 1966. Television.

Kipling, Rudyard. "If." *Wikipedia, the Free Encyclopedia.* Web. 15 Nov. 2007.

Knox, David, Ph. D., and Caroline Schacht. *Heartchoice.com.* MA, Web Hosts, 2004. Knox Enterprises. Web. 2 Jul. 2004.

Kornfield, Jack. *Teachings of the Buddha.* New York: Barnes & Noble Books, 1993. Print.

Kramer vs. Kramer. Dir. Robert Benton. Perf. Dustin Hoffman, Meryl Streep, Jane Alexander, and Justin Henry. Columbia Tristar, 1979. Film.

Larsen, Douglas. "Abuse/Incest Support: Why Women Return-Why Do Women Return?" *About.com.* About, Inc., 2004. Web. 18 Feb. 2004.

Lem, Sharon. "Breakups Traumatic for Teens." *Toronto Sun News* 15 Feb. 2004, General News. Canoe. Web. 27 June 2004.

Lewis, Jone Johnson. *WisdomQuotes.com.* 1995-2003. Web. 26 June 2004.

Works Cited

Linehan, Marsha. *Skills Training Manual for Treating Borderline Personality Disorder*. New York: The Guilford Press, 1993. Print.

Loftus, Elizabeth F. "Memory." *World Book Online Reference Center*. Feb. 2004. World Book, Inc. Web. 1 Feb. 2004.

Lozoff, Bo. *An Evening with Bo Lozoff*. Human Kindness Foundation, 1990. Videocassette.

Lozoff, Bo. *The Dharma of Family Life*. Bo Lozoff: Human Kindness Foundation, 1997. Audiocassette.

Lozoff Bo. *Human Kindness Foundation*. Personal Interview. 1992.

Lozoff, Bo. *It's Not the Top, It's the Climb*. Durham: Human Kindness Foundation, 1998. Print.

Lozoff, Bo. *Just Another Spiritual Book*. Durham: Human Kindness Foundation, 1991. Print.

Lozoff, Bo. *KLOS Radio Interview*. Human Kindness Foundation, 1991. Audiocassette.

Lozoff, Bo. *Past the Boiling Point*. Durham: Human Kindness Foundation, 2002. Print.

Lozoff, Bo. *Talks & Discussions with Bo Lozoff*. Bo Lozoff: Human Kindness Foundation, 1988-89. Audiocassette.

Lozoff, Bo. *We're All Doing Time*. Durham: Human Kindness Foundation, 1984. Print.

Lozoff Sita. *Human Kindness Foundation*: Telephone Interview. 2002.

Manscen. *Prayer of Saint Francis, The*. 17 May 2004. Web. 26 June 2004.

MartialArtsPlanet.com. Web. 2 Dec. 2004.

Martin, Kelly. "Traitors in American History." *About.com*. About, Inc., 2004. Web. 28 June 2004.

Mayer, Richard W. Ph. D., Professor of Psychology. *Psy 200 Unit 4*. 19 April 2003. San Francisco State University. Web. 27 June 2004.

Memory Lifter.com. 10 Nov. 2003. MemoryLifter.com. Web. 27 June 2004.

MentalHealth.com. Web. 19 Nov 2004.

"Mental Illness." *World Book Online Reference Center*. Feb. 2004. World Book, Inc. Web. 1 Feb. 2004.

Merriam-Webster Collegiate Dictionary: Eleventh Edition. Springfield, MA: Merriam-Webster, Inc., 2003. Print.

Messsina, James J., and Constance Messina. *Coping.Org Tools for Coping with Life's Stressors: Tools for Personal Growth*. 1999-2004. James J. Messina, Ph. D. & Constance Messina, Ph. D. Web. 2 Feb. 2004.

Miracosta.cc.ca.us. Web. 27 June 2004.

Works Cited

Misery. Dir. Rob Reiner. Perf. James Caan, Kathy Bates, Lauren Bacall, Richard Farnsworth, and Frances Sternhagen. Columbia Pictures, 1990. Film.

Nami.org. Web. 19 Nov 2004.

Narcotics Anonymous. *Recovery and Relapse*. Van Nuys, CA: Narcotics Anonymous World Services, Inc., 1986. Print.

Narcotics Anonymous. *Self-Acceptance*. Van Nuys, CA: Narcotics Anonymous World Services, Inc., 1986. Print.

New Living Translation: New Testament with Psalms and Proverbs. The Netherlands: Tyndale Charitable Trust, 1996. Print.

New World Translation of the Holy Scriptures. New York: Watchtower Bible and Tract Society of New York, Inc., 1984. Print.

New York Times.com. 2004. The New York Times Company. Web. 12 Dec. 2004.

Ojar.com. 2003-2004. Ojar, LLC. Web. 25 Aug 2004.

Osmosis@usc.edu. Web. 13 July 2004.

Pacificnet.net. Web. 4 Dec. 2004.

Peaches.com,, The. Web. 8 Jul. 2004.

Pearsall, Paul, Ph. D. *The Heart's Code*. New York: Broadway Books, 1998. Print.

Pearsall, Paul, Ph. D. *The Pleasure Prescription: To Love, to Work, to Play-Life in the Balance*. Alameda, California: Hun House Publishers, 1996. Print.

Piper, John. *The Passion of Jesus Christ*. Wheaton: Crossway Books, 2004. Print.

PrimalPage.com. Web. 26 June 2004.

PsychicJournal.com. Web. 24 Dec 2004.

Psycho. Dir. Alfred Hitchcock. Perf. Anthony Perkins, Janet Leigh, and Vera Miles. Universal Studios, 1960. *Psycho.Html*. Web. 12 Dec. 2004.

"Puppy Love." The Osmonds. MGM, 1972. *Quotations Index*. Web. 27 June 2004.

QuotationsPage.com. 1994-2004. The Quotations Page. Web. 27 June 2004.

Quoteland.com. 1997-2001. Quoteland.com. Web. 28 June 2004.

QuotesandJokes.com. Web. 14 Aug. 2004.

Quoteworld.org. Web. 28 June 2004.

Ravensbranch.Allen.com. Web. 19 Aug. 2004.

Works Cited

Regarding Henry. Dir. Mike Nichols. Perf. Harrison Ford, Annette Bening, Rebecca Miller, Bruce Altman, Donald Moffat and Bill Nunn. Paramount Pictures, 1991. Film.

Rejesus.co. 2003. Web. 20 Nov. 2004.

"Remembering Not to Forget." *World Book OnLine Reference Center*. 2004. World Book, Inc. Web. 1 Feb. 2004.

Rifkin, Arthur, MD. "Compassion Personified." *Friends Journal* (2002): 14-15. Print.

Rosenthal, Morris. *FonerBooks.com*. 2001. Web. 28 June 2004.

Roswell, Florence G. and Gladys Natchez. *Reading Disability: A Human Approach to Evaluation and Treatment of Reading and Writing Difficulties*. New York: Basic Books, Inc., 1989. Print.

Shining, The. Dir. Stanley Kubrick. Perf. Jack Nicholson, Shelley Duvall, Scatman Crothers Barry Nelson and Danny Lloyd. Warner Bros., 1980. Film.

Simply Scripts.com. 1999-2003. Simply Scripts. Web. 12 Dec. 2004.

Smith, Wigglesworth. *Nemontel.net*. Web. 31 Aug.

Spanoudis, Stephen. *The OtherPages.org*. 1994-2003. Web. 28 June 2004.

Staton, John., CSW. Personal Interview. 2 Feb 2004.

"Stockholm Syndrome, The." *The Peace Encyclopedia*. 2002. Yahoodi Communications. Web. 18 Feb. 2004.

"Stockholm Syndrome." *World Book Online*. 2004. World Book, Inc. Web. 18 Feb. 2004.

Stone, Greg. *SouthCoastToday.com*. 4 June 1995. Web. 18 Feb. 2004.

SylviasPlace.com. 2001. Sylviasplace.com. Web. 28 June 2004.

T., Buddy. "Alcoholism/Substance Abuse: Domestic Abuse-A Victim Speaks-Women Can Be Batterers, Too." *About.com*. About, Inc., 2004. Web. 18 Feb. 2004.

T., Buddy. "Alcoholism/Substance Abuse: Domestic Abuse-Why Do They Do It?" *About.com*. About, Inc., 2004. Web. 18 Feb. 2004.

Ten Commandments. The. Dir. Cecil B. De Milles. Perf. Charlton Heston, Yul Brynner, Ivonne DeCarlo, Anne Baxter, Debra Paget, Sir Cedric Hardwicke, John Derek, Nina Foch, John Carradine, Edward G. Robinson, and Vincent Price. Paramount Pictures, 1956.

ThinkExist.com. 1999-2004. Think Exist. Web. 9 July 2004.

TimeforHope.org. Web. 2 Dec. 2004.

Tyler, Anne. *The Accidental Tourist*. New York: Knopf: Distributed by Richard House, 1985. Print.

Video.com. Web. 27 Aug. 2004.

Works Cited

View to a Kill, A. Dir. John Glen. Perf. Roger Moore, Christopher Walken, Tanya Roberts, and Grace Jones. MGM, 1985. Film.

iVillage.co.uk. 2000-2004. iVillage UK Limited. 1995-2004. Ivillage, Inc. Web. 2 Jul. 2004.

Watts, Alan. *The Wisdom of Insecurity*. New York: Pantheon Books, 1951. Print.

Webfitz.com. Web. 13 July 2004.

Webster, Richard. *Richard Webster.net*. 2002. Web. 28 June 2004.

Webster's New World Dictionary and Thesaurus: Second Edition. Hungry Minds, Inc., New York: 2002. Print.

Weisstein, Eric W. "Young Girl-Old Woman Illusion." From *Math World*-A Wolfram Web Resource, 2004.

Willford, Jennifer. *LifeSkillsIntl.org*. Webmaster. 2002. Cyspace City. Web. 13 July 2004.

Womanabuseprevention.com. Web. 28 June 2004.

4Woman.gov. March 2003. Web. 13 July 2004.

"Young Man with a Horn." *The Honeymooners*. Dumont Electronicam T-V Film System. Jackie Gleason Enterprises, Inc. Productions Park Sheraton Hotel, New York City, NY 10 Mar. 1955. Television.

Zimmerman, Mark. "Dictionary Information: Definition Deceit." *SelfKnowledge.com*. 1999-2001. Web. 18 Feb. 2004.

Index